T0208729

TRUST THE PROCESS

A SIMPLE—BUT NOT EASY—PATH TO GREATNESS

TIFFANY WAITE CROSBY

WESTBOW
PRESS®
A DIVISION OF THOMAS NELSON
& ZONDERVAN

WestBow Press books may be ordered through booksellers or by contacting:

WestBow Press
A Division of Thomas Nelson & Zondervan
1663 Liberty Drive
Bloomington, IN 47403
www.westbowpress.com
1 (866) 928-1240

ISBN: 978-1-9736-5444-5 (sc)
ISBN: 978-1-9736-5446-9 (hc)
ISBN: 978-1-9736-5445-2 (e)

Library of Congress Control Number: 2019902870

Print information available on the last page.

WestBow Press rev. date: 03/08/2019

ACKNOWLEDGMENTS

The power of affirming words timely spoken is beyond description. I wouldn't have written my first book without them. And without that first book, there would be no second book (or third or fourth). Without affirmation, I wouldn't have had the courage to push forward with becoming a pastor within the Assemblies of God. Without affirmation, I couldn't have begun to share the painful moments that I share within this second book. I'm privileged to have a strong, vibrant community supporting me in whatever way needed. I couldn't begin to list all the people who have affirmed me since that first book was written, but they know who they are, so to all of them I say thank you. Thank you for continuing to express your love for me in both word and deed. Thank you for delivering an encouraging word or a listening ear when I needed it. Thank you for just being you, day in and day out.

If any of you reading this acknowledgment do not have this positive influence in your life, I pray that will change. I pray that words of life will be spoken over you and that the greatness that lies within you will be called forth. I pray that you will become a part of a vibrant, life-giving community and that you will sow as much (if not more) than you reap from being a part of that community. I pray that the hardness of life is softened by the joy of fellowship and friendship. As one who was a loner as a child and young adult, I can say it's never too late to engage in community. So to all of those who have grafted me into your life, thank you. I appreciate it more than words can say.

CONTENTS

CHAPTER 8

APPENDIX 1

APPENDIX 2

PREFACE

On July 1, 2007, I arrived—or so I thought. It was the day that I officially became an executive director at Ernst and Young (EY), a global professional services firm. For those of you not familiar with professional services firms, there are positional hierarchies that resemble a triangle. The first two levels in a firm are often titled staff and senior; these levels roughly equate to one to five years of experience. Leadership at the staff level is primarily focused on leading self. At the senior level, you may also provide guidance and oversight to staff and seniors with less experience. But once you reach the manager level, your leadership responsibilities significantly increase. You begin to lead teams. You also take on leadership responsibilities within the organization and within the community. You may sit on committees and boards of nonprofit organizations, and you may get tapped to train staff and seniors. This is also where the ranks begin to thin out. You do not need as many managers as you do seniors, and so regardless of performance, every senior will not become a manager.

The ranks thin out again at the senior manager level. Senior managers own portfolios of accounts, which mean that they're responsible for everything that happens within those accounts. They need to make sure clients are happy and that the work gets done on time, within budget, and with the right level of quality. They also have to sell more work so that all those staff, seniors, and managers have work to do. And they have to manage all the people stuff like performance reviews, recruiting, and staff development. If you're successful at that level, then you might progress to the next level of leadership, which is basically either a partner or executive director. So when I became an executive director, I felt like my hard work had been rewarded. I had achieved my vision of success and life would now be easy - or so I thought.

I will never forget the voicemail from our chairman and CEO that awaited me and all those newly promoted to partner, principal, or executive director. After congratulating us on reaching such a significant milestone in our careers, he went on to counsel us about the responsibilities we had as part of the executive leadership team. He cautioned us that everything we did now reflected upon the firm; there was no such thing as off-the-record behavior. We were the face and voice of EY. We were to represent EY well twenty-four seven. We were to give thought to what message our actions or communications would send if blasted on the front page of the *Wall Street Journal* or subjected to inspection in the courtroom. If there was ever a question of integrity as it related to a course of action, we were to stop, think, and consult. No person or company was more important than the reputation of the firm; it had been built over many lifetimes but could be destroyed in moment. I'm more than ten years removed from that message but remember it like it was yesterday. Though directed to those being welcomed into the executive leadership team, it truly is a message relevant to all leaders. Reputations are slowly built but quickly destroyed. I felt good when I listened to that message. I was ready for whatever challenges would come my way—or so I thought.

When I listened to that message, I listened as one expecting my greatest challenges to come from the external world. I expected that I would have to hold difficult conversations with clients and staff. In my profession, consultants are often the bearers of bad news. I knew I would have to make difficult decisions; it's part of business. What I didn't know was that we were about to head into murky economic waters. I did not see the economic downturn coming that would force us into multiple rounds of staffing cuts. I didn't expect to have to inform people that their jobs no longer existed. I knew

I would be challenged to develop new relationships, secure new business, and deliver exceptional service. What I didn't know was that I would be challenged to do this while companies were cutting spending, delaying investments, abandoning any projects deemed non-mission critical, and generally trying to stay afloat. Still, with all those unexpected challenges, what really surprised me most was not the pressure created by external circumstances but rather the internal struggle I would encounter. Business leadership, though mentally and emotionally exhausting, didn't require me to confront my personal values, beliefs, and attitudes, as well as the thoughts and actions they drove. I could build business and build a name for myself without ever stopping to work on me. I could do all the right things and be successful at doing them without being successful at being. What I didn't realize was that this success would be empty.

When things came crashing down on me, I was not prepared. I was not prepared to face the challenges that would come from within me. I was in no way prepared for the junk that would surface once I had achieved a certain measure of success, influence, and financial means. I couldn't have imagined that I was even capable of making some of the decisions that I made, a few of which could have ruined my family, my career, and my life. I was not prepared for the stuff that I would see as I took a holistic perspective to life and began to inspect my values, assumptions, and beliefs. There were no secular (i.e., non-Christian) leadership books that could prepare me for the character deficits that would become so obvious to me once I stripped away the veneer. There was an ugliness that lay beneath a beautiful exterior, and it began to rise to the surface, as it does with many people caught up in material success, power, and influence. Deep within, there was a person who was more selfish than I could've ever imagined and who was determined to have it her way regardless of the cost. That person took me on a detour that almost cost me my life and could've hurt a lot of people in the process. I emerged from that time stronger, more grounded, and solidified within my leadership like never before. I know who I am and what I stand for because I had to battle it out in the trenches. I had to search deep. I had to deconstruct lies that I had believed and didn't even realize I had believed them. I had to confront old pains and hurts that were buried so deep that I didn't know they were there, yet they were holding me in bondage and shaping how I led.

For far too long, we've had an arbitrary separation between business (the marketplace) effectiveness and spiritual wholeness, as if we can actually separate what we believe to be true about ourselves and others from the decisions we make and how we lead. We've also worked hard to convince people that individual worth and greatness is measured by what you do instead of who you are. We've peddled the lie that great leadership is about displaying certain leadership skills such as critical thinking, business acumen, and communication skills rather than character development. I beg to differ. I had great leadership skills even when I had severe character deficits, and they did propel me to a certain level of material success, but the cost was great. That's what I want to explore with you in this book.

I did not write this book because we need another book on leadership or personal transformation. I wrote this book because the pain of the process I went through demanded expression. This isn't a book about getting everything right. This is a book about redeemed failure and the lessons learned along the way. It's also a book about human possibilities and the fact that these possibilities live on even when we get off track because there's an immeasurable amount of grace available to us. It's also a book about learning to live intentionally so that you're able to take a straight path toward greatness instead of having to course correct later on. Writing this book was emotionally draining. I cried a lot as I relived some of the life moments shared throughout the book. I struggled with how much detail to include about my own challenges. I wondered how I could have been so deceived while also marveling at how far I had come. But in the end, there was a feeling of deep satisfaction in bringing to light all that had occurred under the surface. I suppose you can say that I trusted the process of character development that is the entire premise of this book.

I hope that you will likewise walk away from the time you spend reading this book positively changed. May the wanderings of my soul, the contemplations of my mind, and the stories of my life inspire you to commit to the life of greatness meant for you.

INTRODUCTION

When you look back on history and think of those who have accomplished great feats that have redefined society in a positive way, who comes to mind? Within more modern times, I think of William Wilberforce, Abraham Lincoln, Mother Teresa, Nelson Mandela, and Mahatma Gandhi, to name of few. These are great men and women of courage who fought against established social structures to make lasting changes. Their battles weren't easy or short. They experienced hardships in their lives, some caused by external circumstances outside of their control and others created by their attempts to live in accordance with their internal convictions. There were parts of their lives that weren't pretty. Whether it was lavish living, paying bribes, romantic entanglements, or other actions that many would deem inconsistent with sound character, they all had issues to overcome. They also made mistakes along the way, some of which would have seemed to preclude them from positions of leadership. All had to draw away at some point to understand who they were and what they believed. And once they did, they had to confront societal beliefs that didn't align with their core values. When it comes to influential individuals whom we deeply respect, it's easy for us to focus on the endgame. We can get enamored with the final results and assume that the person was always that way. I've never found that to be the case. Every person of great character has gone through a process of development from which we can learn. If we are to really understand what it takes to be great, we will have to go beyond the end of their lives. We'll have to dig a lot deeper to understand the life circumstances and situations that became a training and development ground for them, as well as examine the patterns that emerge.

William Wilberforce labored for forty-six years to abolish the British slave trade. He aired his petition year after year only to be rejected, but he kept coming back. He was mocked and ridiculed. He found himself on the wrong side of business—the slave trade was quite profitable. He was far from the best friend of high society because they too benefited significantly from the slave trade. Yet he kept at it for forty-six years. He persevered because he believed in the righteousness of his cause and understood the nature of social change. He realized that social change happens when the hearts and minds of people are changed, and that doesn't happen overnight. I'm sure he would've liked for it to happen in less time than it did, but he stayed the course nonetheless.

How was he able to endure the difficulties associated with being a change agent for such a long period of time? What type of character does it take to patiently labor for five decades to see a dream become a reality? History remembers his greatness, but as we so often do, we forget or gloss over the struggle that led up to it.

William Wilberforce lost his father when he was nine and was sent to live with rich aunts and uncles. After inheriting his uncle's wealth, he went to Cambridge, where he immersed himself in an indulgent lifestyle—playing cards, attending the theatre, and dining with the best foods and wine. He was prescribed opium for his digestive health issues which ultimately made him more careless and haphazard. He was deemed unfit to hold any important position in government. This hardly sounds like the profile of the man who would fight to abolish the British slave trade. What happened? At what point did William Wilberforce develop the inner conviction and character necessary to champion such an unpopular cause? For Wilberforce, it began as all great transformations do: with recognition that he was spiritually broken and needed correction. His leadership, for which he is now lauded, didn't begin with a leadership development course; it began with coming face-to-face with who he really was spiritually and then deciding that he no longer wanted to go down that course. At that point, he became sensitive to the plight of the poor. One thing led to another, and the William Wilberforce we know and celebrate emerged.

Abraham Lincoln is viewed as one of the country's most pivotal historical leaders because he led the country through a civil war to abolish the American slave trade and established the foundation for the reunification of the divided country. Although he wouldn't see this reunification through because of his untimely assassination, the structures he had begun to put in place paved the way for his successor. However, Abraham Lincoln's life was anything but easy, and his career was a mixed bag of successes and failures. His mother died when he was still young—a traumatic event for any child. He worked on the family farm until he decided to launch out on his own. He immediately met with failure because the business that he began to work for went out of business, leaving him unemployed. His first attempts in politics weren't much to write home about; he failed to receive the nomination that he coveted. He was a failed businessman and a failed politician, and nothing within that resume would lead you to believe that he would become one of the greatest presidents the United States has had. He met with failure over and over again, yet he was not deterred from his goal.

In contrast to William Wilberforce, the character traits of Abraham Lincoln that we've come to know and love were formed when he was quite young. Biographies are full of accounts of his deep, genuine care for people and their stories from a young age. He seemed to have an incredible gift of empathy. He was generally liked by all who met him, was humble enough to do whatever work needed done for whoever needed it, and earned people's trust quite quickly. His integrity seems to be without question no matter what account you read. Even his political enemies didn't have complaints that they could raise against him other than a lack of experience and an unwillingness to put on airs. What you saw was what you got. The most cited character traits for Abraham Lincoln are truth, candor, forthrightness, resiliency, and charitableness. In Lincoln, we see a different aspect of character development. He had the character to lead from a young age. Yet his road to a position of influence was still quite long and met with many failures. His transformation was different than Wilberforce's transformation, yet it was just as vital to his long-term success. His dogged perseverance was forged as he continued to press on, and through hard work he became a lawyer and the president of the United States. What drove Lincoln to continue despite all the setbacks? Could there have been a purpose served by those setbacks? Just imagine the amount of perseverance he had developed by the path he had to take and how that would play out during a civil war that tore a nation apart. How many opportunities do you think Lincoln had to compromise? How many of his political advisers counseled him to be a bit more diplomatic so that the war could end? After all, the costs were pretty high in both lives and resources. Who wouldn't want to bring an end to the carnage? Yet persevere he did, and our history has been forever altered because of it.

Similarly, Mother Teresa is known for laboring endlessly to care for the poor and the needy and the outcast. She wasn't afraid to go where others dared not tread, and she wasn't afraid to touch those labeled as untouchable. Neither people living in leper colonies nor those living in tuberculosis wards were off-limits to her. Like Abraham Lincoln, Mother Teresa also experienced the loss of a parent (her father) at a young age (nine years old). Her sensitivities to the plight of others would begin to develop as she became more exposed to their stories through her mother. Though this empathy was an important piece of the equation, there was still more to develop in Mother Teresa before the woman we have come to know is truly born. Setting out from her Macedonian home to become a missionary at the age of eighteen, Mother Theresa would spend approximately one year in Ireland before heading to India. She would take her first religious vows as a nun two years later and her solemn vows six years after that. She would spend almost twenty years in total as a teacher at a convent school before becoming its headmistress. This school, though close to the slums, was comprised of primarily wealthy students. She would act in the headmistress role for almost four years before leaving the school to follow her calling to the mission's field of helping the poor. She had spent a long time observing the poor in India prior to leaving the convent to serve them. Did this time serve a purpose? Could this time possibly have been a part of her development process rather than idle years spent teaching students of privilege?

We are prone to remember the later years of her life, but how much do we reflect on the twenty-five-year journey between leaving home and setting out to serve the poor? How quick are we to celebrate the struggles that ultimately led to the success that she would later experience? Mother Theresa's life wasn't easy, and it wasn't without controversies, but it was significant. There were times when patients couldn't be helped, and they died in the care of the sisters. Some leaders would later question the quality of care received in their home and the focus placed on baptism of those who were dying, with a few publishing rather scathing reviews. People were attracted to her cause, which meant that some people who donated had less than stellar reputations. Questions of guilt by association and improprieties would surface and continue long after Mother Teresa's death in 1997. As her life was studied more, personal writings would reveal a struggle with loneliness and feeling disconnected from God. She didn't always feel as close to God as she did as a young novice, and felt her zeal waning. This is not an uncommon struggle for individuals operating on the fringes. Though her name would become synonymous with compassion through hard work over a long period of time, her life was not carefree and her character was not beyond reproach. She made mistakes, as we all do. She took chances, as we all must. Some would work out, and some would not, as is always the case. Her good choices would be celebrated. Her poor choices would be critiqued, as is common for public celebrities. It's easy to get caught up in all these arguments, but if you do, you lose sight of the bigger picture. You lose sight of the length of her journey, the depths of her struggles, and the strength and fortitude necessary to stay the course. You lose sight of the character development process that was occurring throughout her life.

Then you have Nelson Mandela. Mandel was imprisoned for twenty-seven years under an apartheid system. By the world's standards, he would have every right to be bitter and seek revenge on those who had mistreated him, separated him from his family, and robbed him of almost three decades of freedom. Who would've thought that his modeling forgiveness would pave the way forward for him to lead the nation that oppressed him toward recovery and healing? What would have happened to South Africa had Mandela not put the needs of the people ahead of any personal desire for retribution? Can you imagine what the nation and the world might look like today had he modeled a different path? His accomplishments as the leader of a post-apartheid nation that desperately needed to move forward are impressive. Coming out of prison, Mandela had a choice as to how to wield his influence and authority. He could use it to divide the nation, calling for revenge and an uprising—or he could use it to unite the nation.

During his time in prison, Mandela was at the mercy of the prison guards. They had the power to make his life miserable, and judging from written accounts, they chose to do so on occasion. So why did Mandela choose unity instead of the revenge? What within his character allowed him to make that choice and how was it developed? What role did the circumstances of his life play within that development? How did both his successes and failures contribute to the man who would win the Nobel Peace Prize in 1993? Upon the death of his father when Nelson was only twelve, he became ward of the acting king of his tribe, because his father had been the principal counsellor for this king. He was well schooled during his primary and secondary years, but he was expelled from college for participating in a student protest. Threatened with an arranged marriage if he chose to not return to school, Nelson ran away to Johannesburg, South Africa, and took a job as a mine security officer. Through a series of circumstantial meetings, Nelson would ultimately complete his bachelor's of arts degree and began pursuing his bachelor's of law, a degree he'd never finish. Choosing to leave this pursuit, Nelson would instead decide to engage in politics. With his legal background, he was able to establish the first black-owned law firm in South Africa. His political aggressiveness would also increase. A political strike was threatened but ultimately called off. Retreat was only temporary because Nelson gathered forces, obtained military training, and prepared to come back stronger. It's this path that would ultimately lead him down the path of imprisonment and ultimately to leadership of a nation freed from the weight of apartheid.

There's nothing about this story that would suggest that Nelson would emerge from prison seeking peace instead of taking up arms. He had already paid a high price in that his family was no longer by his side (a wife and two daughters) and he had lost his freedom. What more was there for him to lose? But something happened in that prison as he interacted with those guards on a daily basis, and as he reflected upon the purpose and meaning in life. A man was born in that prison who hadn't existed before and whom the nation desperately needed. There's nothing fair or just about the sentence Nelson received or the treatment he endured. Yet as we'll see throughout this book, our response to difficult circumstances is one of the key determining factors in our character development process. Leaders do not achieve what they do because they are free from difficult circumstances; rather, they achieve what they do because they allow those difficult circumstances to teach and instruct them in powerful ways.

We see this power at work in Mahatma Gandhi, perhaps the most controversial of the figures whom I've noted. Mahatma Gandhi used civil disobedience to inspire the British-ruled India toward independence. His actions have inspired many in their push for civil rights and freedoms across the world. Gandhi was born in 1869 but did not begin his work in India until 1915, at the age of forty-six, after having been trained in law in London and working as an expatriate lawyer in South Africa. His start in India was not the stuff of history books. It really began with organizing peasants, farmers, and urban laborers to protest excessive land-tax and discrimination. His influence would grow as he assumed leadership of the Indian National Congress and took on issues involving poverty, women's rights, and abolishment of the untouchable caste. His early childhood didn't have some of the challenges that we see in the stories of others profiled. His father served as a prime minister to several India states. His mother was a deeply religious woman, raising Gandhi in Hinduism and Jainism with a regular schedule of meditation and fasting. He was married at thirteen in an arranged marriage, to which he rebelled by smoking, eating meat, and stealing change. With an expectation that he would follow in his father's footsteps, he was sent to London at the age of eighteen (shortly after the birth of his first son) to study law. Returning to India three years later, Gandhi thought he was prepared to enter law, but his first case was a disaster. Gandhi blanked when he went to cross-examine his first witness, and he fled the courtroom. After struggling to find work in India, he left to go to South Africa on a one-year contract to provide legal services.

It was in South Africa that he became appalled at the discrimination and racial segregation faced by Indian immigrants. Gandhi's first act of civil disobedience wasn't planned. He simply refused to move from the first-class compartment to the back of the train at the complaint of a white man who was offended by his presence, though he had a valid ticket. Gandhi would go on to start the Natal Indian Congress and raise up an all-Indian ambulance corps to help support the British in the Boer War, all while running a thriving legal practice in South Africa. His first major civil disobedience campaign was launched in South Africa. It was only after this campaign that he was sent back to India. It's his work in India that we remember, but would Gandhi have been as effective if he hadn't taken the time to study law? Would he have had the influence or reach necessary if he hadn't practiced in South Africa? Where would India be today if Gandhi hadn't experienced discrimination firsthand in South Africa? What if Gandhi had been unwilling to start small?

When we examine each of these individuals through a lens of character development and leadership, we will see four glaring commonalities.

First, the accomplishments that we speak of so glowingly did not rise up overnight. They were nurtured and developed over many years of hard work. Forty-six years of persistent pursuit, twenty-seven years of imprisonment, or twenty-five years of seeking God before being called out to the mission field for a lifetime of good deeds and charitable service. These individuals were not after fifteen minutes of fame, which is a good thing because notoriety was often experienced before honor. They were not striving for wealth. Instead, they were motivated by something greater: a sense of purpose that transcended themselves. They had to be in order to go the distance. They had to have some greater purpose in order to withstand disappointments, difficulties, and persecution. What might have happened if William Wilberforce had decided that he had been rejected enough times, and it was time to cut his losses and move on to an issue that he could win? What if he had decided to champion an issue that was more popular than ending the British slave trade? What if he soothed his conscience and sense of morality by saying he'd done what he could, and nothing more should be expected of him? After all, he was lobbying for ending a practice that was an economic boom for Britain. That is not the way to win popularity votes. Can you imagine what our world might look like today had he not been willing to risk his reputation, his social and political standing, and his relationships? He indeed accomplished a great work and made a name for himself, but not because that was his goal. Greatness was not his pursuit, but it was the outcome.

Second, these individuals were passionately committed to that purpose. They didn't let failure hold them back. Abraham Lincoln could've decided that politics wasn't for him after his first or second unsuccessful attempt. Instead, he continued with dogmatic tenaciousness until he became president of the United States at a perilous time in the nation's history. What would have happened if Abraham Lincoln had decided that he had invested enough time and energy, and it was time to move on to something else more suited to him? What might our history look like with an American president who was unwilling to deal with the darkness that had engulfed the nation in the form of slavery? The Civil War was costly. In today's dollars, the war would have cost roughly $2.5 million daily; the estimated final cost is $6.2 billion. This does not include the incalculable cost of lost lives, the devastation to Southern cities, or the broken family relationships as brother fought against brother. Yet it was a war that had to be fought. How much longer might the institution of American slavery have lasted without his willingness to stay the course? Can you imagine what our world might look like today had he taken the easy path of leadership and not risked his reputation, his social and political standing, and his relationships? The great work Abraham Lincoln accomplished was not a result of his doing but of his being. He had the character to lead, and because of that, he achieved greatness. Greatness was not his pursuit, but it was the outcome.

Third, each person matured over time into the character we now admire. Mother Teresa lost her father when she was only nine years old. This loss would start her on the path of compassion as she grew closer to her mother who was deeply committed to charity. Yet, it wasn't until after teaching in India for seventeen years to privileged kids on the outskirts of the slums that the compassion needed to devote herself to caring for the sick and the poor had fully taken root. Her order would ultimately start hospices, leper colonies, and schools for the blind, deaf, and poor. Yet it wasn't until October 7, 1950, twenty-one years after arriving in India, that Mother Teresa received Vatican permission to start the diocesan congregation that would become the Missionaries of Charity. Its mission was to care for "the hungry, the naked, the homeless, the crippled, the blind, the lepers, all those people who feel unwanted, unloved, uncared for throughout society, people that have become a burden to the society and are shunned by everyone," as she noted in her Nobel Peace Prize acceptance in 1979. Had Mother Teresa not waited, had she not been willing to serve where she was placed until the doors opened, and had she rushed the process, would she have had tenacity she needed to get the results that we so admire? Would she have grown weary from the toll of compassion? A deeply rooted, unshakable commitment is necessary to go where no one else would go, to care for those no one else would care for without regard to reputation, safety, or personal needs. Without this compassion, would there be over 760 Missionaries of Charity houses located in over 139 countries around the world? That number excludes the additional sects and branches that have sprung up as well. Can you imagine the world without the charity that is done by these missionaries? Had Mother Teresa looked for the quick fix, the easy solution, or the magic bullet, we wouldn't be reading about her today. Her life was lived one plodding moment to the next, as is so often the case with those who achieve greatness. Looking at it in the rearview mirror can seem magical; living it is anything but.

Fourth, these people had moments of truth in their lives where they had to examine what they believed and whether they were leading their lives in accordance with what they believed. Signing the Emancipation Proclamation was a moment of truth for Abraham Lincoln. It was the ultimate test of his character. Was he willing to stand behind what he believed to be true about the dignity of human life? Was he willing to take an action that he knew would ultimately lead the nation to war? Once William Wilberforce accepted Christ as Savior, learned the truth of the gospel, and became awakened to the plight of the poor, he had to ask himself whether he was willing to give up his good name, his social standing, and his easy life to stand on what he believed. When great destinies are at stake, character will always be tested. Mother Teresa had many moments where she could've walked away from serving the poor in India and made lots of money from what she had already accomplished. Was she willing to trade in her calling for material wealth? When societal norms are being confronted and transformational change is being introduced, conviction will always be tested. Greatness, as defined later in this book, will always demand sacrifice and resiliency.

If we were to examine the lives of other great men and women of history, we'd see that their greatness was not achieved overnight. The road to greatness is one that is traveled over an extended period of time. It's full of hills and valleys, twists and turns, and many opportunities to prematurely off-ramp. Unfortunately, the road is also full of alluring detours that can permanently sidetrack you or, if you're lucky, merely delay you from your reaching your destination. There is a process that leads to the development of character the likes of which we see in these great men and women of history. If we're to achieve the greatness that is meant for us, then we need to undergo this process. Although it's nice to understand the process, it's even more important that you trust it so that you don't shortcut it. If you shortcut the process, you will shortcut the results.

Mother Teresa went through this process up until her dying breath. Though she received many offers for books, movies, and documentaries and was routinely nominated to receive awards, some of which carried cash prizes, she never let this fame derail her from her purpose. She could've used the fame to live a more comfortable life. She could've justified slowing down a bit and enjoying her retirement years. Instead, she chose to stay true to her God-given purpose. Where did she get such resolve? How did she have the strength and tenacity to live in a very countercultural way—and do so in a way that garnered the respect of the world? Although we can only read between the lines of her individual story, I've studied enough biographies to know that greatness is forged when people willingly undergo a process of character development. Mother Teresa's character development started as a child, continued throughout her life, and followed a rather predictable process. Had she chosen to short-change the process, we probably wouldn't be reading about her or celebrating her contributions to society.

Every great person worthy of studying underwent a process of growth and development. These people did not start out as world-renowned leaders. They met with failure and had to overcome it. They had to learn discipline and empathy and how to properly use their influence. They had to determine their true values and what they were willing to sacrifice to live in accordance with them. They had to break away from the superficial measures used by the world to define success, and they tapped into something greater that would keep them properly focused and motivated over the long haul. The process they underwent was slow and methodical. At times it may have even seemed like they were going backward instead of forward. Their stories are fun to read. Their lives are inspirational. We hold them up as examples of what is possible, forgetting about the process they had to go through to get there. So we wonder whether it's possible for us to influence our world to that same magnitude. We ask those questions because we've glamorized their lives. We've made them mystical and magical, as if Abraham Lincoln was born with presidential genes that asserted themselves once he reached a certain age. But that is not what happened. Each person underwent a process—a process that is available to each and every one of us, if we're willing to submit ourselves to it.

A process, by definition, consists of a series of actions or steps taken in order to achieve a desirable end goal. Inherent within this definition of process are three key assumptions of desirability, achievability, and reliability. We assume that the end goal is desired and can be achieved, and that this achievement can occur by following a series of steps. In order to understand how greatness looks and how greatness is achieved, we must understand these assumptions as they relate to processes in general, and then how they relate specifically to greatness.

QUESTION 1: SHOULD YOU DESIRE GREATNESS?

The first assumption inherent in the definition of process is that there is a defined end in mind that is worthy of achieving. In other words, there is a predetermined goal that the person wants to achieve. If the process leads to an end state that is less than desirable, then we have little reason to invest in the process. It's not that we don't trust the process; rather, it's that we don't care about the process. It's not relevant to us. I have zero desire to be a coffee barista. Though I know there's great training out there that has been proven to work, I have no motivation to participate in said training because it's not relevant to me. However, I do want to achieve significance. I don't believe I'm alone in that regard. I also don't believe that significance and great character are competing dichotomies. You can, and should, desire to have both. Desiring significance is not bad, as we'll examine in this book. However, this desire could become distorted and lead to undesirable behaviors and lives. In your chase for significance, you can sacrifice character. We'll also examine how this occurs and what to do if that happens.

QUESTION 2: IS GREATNESS ACHIEVABLE?

The second assumption is that we believe that the goal is achievable. It's hard to trust a process if you don't believe that the end goal is achievable. Why endure the discipline associated with a process if the expected end result is failure? Logically, rationally, it doesn't make sense to invest your time and energy into something that you believe will fail. I once dreamt of competing athletically but soon realized that it wasn't my forte. I wasn't going to be top athlete material regardless of how great of a coach I had. Having watched my sons excel at football and my daughter excel at gymnastics and competitive cheerleading, I know that coaches consistently following a process can greatly accelerate skill development, but they must have something with which to work. The beauty of greatness is that we all have the base elements necessary for achievement. We're all able to develop the right character for leadership, and we're all able to lead in ways that create a lasting impact on our generation and generations to come.

QUESTION 3: CAN I RELY ON THE PROCESS?

The third assumption is that the steps, when followed as prescribed, will lead to the desired end result. Of the three assumptions, this one is the most difficult one to grab hold of within ourselves. We're good at pointing out all that could go wrong. We specialize in identifying obstacles and barriers that appear to be insurmountable roadblocks. We have somehow come to believe that our own ingenuity can take the place of a carefully established process.

As it relates to greatness, my goal in this book is to convince you that:

- Greatness is a goal worthy of achieving; it's desirable
- Greatness is a goal that can be achieved
- There are a series of steps or actions that, when consistently followed, will lead to greatness

The path I propose is simple, but it is not easy. I doubt that this book will introduce new concepts. You will have heard of most, if not all, of these concepts before. However, I also know that knowledge isn't the same as application (or wisdom). Just because you know about them doesn't mean that you know how to effectively apply them in your life, and it doesn't mean that you *are* applying them in your life. I know what a healthy diet looks like, but I don't always eat healthy. There are rather predictable obstacles that often pull me offtrack, such as business travel, social gatherings, and training events. I know what I should do but haven't always employed successful strategies in dealing with these rather predictable situations. Greatness works much the same way.

What that in mind, our goal is not just to look at the principles of greatness but to also deal with the practical realities that so often detour or sidetrack us from following the process. As we explore these principles in a very practical way, we're going to journey through the ups and downs of my life and the lives of a few dear friends. Buckle up if you dare, and let's head out on our journey. We will begin by examining the concept of greatness so that we're all launching out of the same gate.

CHAPTER 1

WHAT IS GREATNESS?

If we looked at the formal definition of greatness, we'd see terms such as *eminence, high standing,* and *distinction.* To be eminent means to be famous or respected within a particular sphere or profession. A person of high standing enjoys a position of rank and the esteem and privileges associated with that rank. A person of distinction has set himself or herself apart from others through accomplishments. Bill Gates and Steve Jobs are respected names within the field of technology. Both were afforded great leeway within the field of technology to introduce innovations; they enjoyed privileges others did not. By the world's standards, they are great men. When thought of in this way, greatness is something that is bestowed on you by others. You're great because the wealth you've amassed, the title you've obtained, or the feats that you've accomplished set you above and apart from others. You've become a point of comparison. People look upon you as a measuring stick of their own greatness.

There are some inherent flaws in this definition of greatness that should make us all uncomfortable. If you settle for this definition of greatness, let me tell you the realities that also await you.

1. What people giveth, they can also take away. Greatness that is bestowed upon you by others can also be taken away by the same people. What may be celebrated, adored, and idolized today may be forgotten or even villainized tomorrow. We see the reality of forgotten heroes played out with athletic superstars, entertainers, and political leaders on a regular basis. Today's star quarterback is tomorrow's has-been as age catches up with him and his passes aren't as accurate or as deep. Singers whose concerts used to sell out as soon as the tickets went on sale now spotlight at second- and third-rate locations to partially filled rooms. Political terms of office come to an end, and your story just isn't interesting anymore. Entourages no longer follow you around. Your opinion isn't sought, and people aren't lining up to pay one thousand dollars a plate to hear you speak. Your star has dimmed.

   We also see the tide of popular opinion change very quickly when moral failures come to light. As a society, we love a juicy story, especially if it involves someone in the limelight. In a perverse sort of way, we enjoy seeing the high and lifted up come tumbling down. In today's hyperconnected society, it takes only a few hours for a video to go viral and the public outrage to begin. People who were once cherished are tried and convicted in the court of popular opinion prior to full discovery of the facts. Reputational damage is done long before a person has his or her rightful day in court.

   Additionally, we like to villainize those who are opposed to popular opinion, regardless of the science, logic, or rationale behind the opposing view. Time may prove them right, but in the short-term they are not very popular. Abolitionists were not popular. Suffrage workers were not celebrated. Today, we look back and admire their courage. We have lifted them up, in many cases long after they've passed on and are no longer around to enjoy the fruits of their labors. But during their day, they were villainized.

If you decide to define greatness based on the adoration of others, you're setting yourself up for disappointment. Someday your star may wane, a defect may surface, or your values may come into conflict with popular opinion, and then your sense of greatness will be gone.

2. There's always someone waiting to dethrone you. If your greatness is based on you holding the record, then be prepared to be toppled off that pedestal. There's always someone waiting in the trenches to accomplish more, to sell more, to operate faster, to innovate, to disrupt, to outshine, to outperform, or to outthink. Think about the sheer number of companies from twenty years ago that don't exist today. Do you remember Blockbuster, Woolworth's, Zayre, or Ames? What about their founders? Can you even remember their names, or have they faded away in your memory? Who uses 8-track players, albums, or CD players? What about floppy disks? The laptops, tablets, and smartphones that we use today are far removed from the first computer. Although that invention set many things into motion, it didn't survive in its original form. Think about all these inventors and how much fame they enjoyed when these items were innovative, hot commodities. Now they're the stuff of historical museums. Even the best of legacies fade over time. Who remembers the valedictorians from Harvard, Princeton, or the other Ivy League schools? To the extent they've managed to achieve some measure of distinction as the world defines it, their names are great trivia for a game night or for competing on *Jeopardy*. But beyond that, their accomplishment is only lifted up by family members, friends, and the employer who chose to hire them. And there will always be the next valedictorian who might have an even higher GPA and go on to greater

heights of accomplishment in the marketplace. Defining greatness based on achievement of a certain measure makes greatness fleeting and causes a constant striving.

3. The greatness beast must be fed. There is a shelf life to accomplishments. What you did today will only be remembered for so long. Eventually the question will become, "What have you done for me lately?" If you can't answer that question, kiss your greatness goodbye. Authors of top-selling business books must release a new book or updated edition every few years to continue to garner demand for speaking events at top-notch rates. Conferences don't want to announce a has-been writer as the keynote speaker. So what happens if you don't release that next book? Your stock drops, and you can no longer demand top dollar. Greatness defined by accomplishments is like a beautiful bouquet of roses cut out of a garden. Their blossoms eventually fade, the petals fall off, and their beauty is lost. The sun has set, the shade has been pulled down, and their best times are behind them.

There is a reason that performance artists must keep producing hits. How many one-hit wonders do you remember? How many actresses and actors do you remember from ten or fifteen years ago? Only the most avid of football fans remembers anyone other than the current record holders. Those who used to hold the rushing record or the touchdown record are forgotten. Greatness that is defined based on what you do instead of who you are will eventually cease to satisfy. It will create an identity crisis at some point in time.

Sadly, we see the same dynamic as it relates to humanitarian disasters. Organizations raising funds for first response are generally successful raising millions of dollars. However, fast-forward one to two years and see how successful those same organizations are at raising funds for the ongoing work. If their leaders get a false sense of hubris based on that initial outpouring, they could be in for a big shock as they see people move on to the next disaster or the next cause. Your cause was important for a while, but attention has now shifted elsewhere. How do you respond to that? If your identity was based on public expression of goodwill and outpouring of support, then you probably won't respond well.

Artificial measures of greatness will trap you on a performance-based Ferris wheel until you either burn out or realize that there is a different measure of greatness that is a peace giver instead of a peace taker. The measure's yoke is easy, and its burden is light. Yes, it requires hard work to achieve because it goes against our very nature, but it is possible. Because this measure of greatness is based not on what you've done but on who you are, it's one that is completely within your control. This measure of greatness focuses on character development. It seeks to ask one very basic question: "Am I the best version of me that I can possibly be?"

There is no competition inherent within this question. Everyone can be great. Wealth is limited; everyone cannot be wealthy. A business only needs one CEO, one CFO, and one chairman of the board. There can be only one award winner in any category. Only one person can hold the world record at a time (barring a tie). Not everyone can go out onto the mission field. Not everyone can be a senior pastor or a community leader. However, everyone can and should be great. Greatness is obtained not by what you do in your life but by how you live. And because it is a factor of life decisions, it's entirely within your grasp.

You have full control over whether you achieve greatness. No one can prevent you from reaching this goal—no one except yourself. Mother Teresa didn't become great because she built hospitals or had buildings or streets named after her. She became great because she had a compassion for the poor that compelled her to action. She lived out her values with passion and perseverance. She couldn't control what the world thought of her; that developed on its own. She could control only how she responded to the misery she saw in front of her. Greatness came to her because she didn't chase the counterfeit symbol of greatness offered by the world. She didn't seek greatness; she sought people. She didn't strive for wealth; she strove to make life better for people. Greatness is a by-product of a life well lived.

I still remember the first time I realized that greatness lies within me. I started my career with only one goal: financial security. I had grown up amid some pretty difficult financial struggles because my mother was widowed when I was eight. I applied myself to my studies because I planned to go to college and knew my mother couldn't afford to send me there; I was going to have to make my own way. I aced my SATs, getting one of the highest scores in our school district. I was awarded academic scholarships to several schools but chose Duquesne University because of the quality of their business school and my ability to commute from home. Majoring in accounting seemed like a logical decision for a person driven by a desire for financial security. However, it doesn't seem so logical when you look at my passion. People's stories have fascinated for as long as I can remember. Historical novels were my fodder when many of my peers were still reading primers. I fell in love with Shakespeare as a teenager. I can't even remember what age I was when I penned my first journal entry or my first poem. Teacher after teacher commented on my gift with language, public speaking, debate, and creative writing. In their minds, I was destined to be a communication major and have a career in political science. When I majored in accounting in college, it didn't make sense to anyone except me. Character development wasn't my motivation. Contributing to society wasn't my motivation. Financial security was my motivation.

I didn't know any CPAs. I didn't know anything about business. However, I did know that my gift of intelligence could easily be applied to the world of business and accounting, and that would provide the launchpad necessary to give me a platform to change my life and my son's life. Although I didn't know the specifics of where an accounting career could take me, I did know that a career in business would feed my desire to travel. I knew I would be exposed to different cultures within Pittsburgh, the United States, and the world at large—if not through the work I did, then through the money I'd make that would allow me to travel the world. And though I didn't know that relationship building would be so critical to my role as my career progressed, I did know that I would have to relate to a lot of other people who didn't share my background. I knew that this career was going to propel me into a world that was foreign to me with people who didn't grow up in my neighborhood and couldn't relate to my struggles. Not only did I not own a suit when I started college, but I didn't own anything that would come close to a professional outfit. I had worked since I was a teenager, but I had never had to create a professional resume or go on a professional interview.

My mind-set when I headed to college was entirely focused on me. Greatness to me was about accomplishment. It was the road to financial security, and that was the road that appealed to me. That was really all that mattered to me. I didn't set out to lead people. I didn't care about leadership; neither did I view myself as having a call to leadership. I knew only that I wanted the power, influence, and financial security that come with positions of leadership, and I knew that a career in business would give me that opportunity far quicker than a career in journalism. I also knew that it would take less time to reach a point of stability in accounting than in any other business career. I didn't have a vision for community. When I graduated summa cum laude, I didn't realize I had accomplished a task achieved by very few blacks (male or female). I was a single mother newly engaged to be married. I was starting a career; there was no thought of other people on my mind. During the early years of my career, my focus was on my family and my own development. I wasn't interested in transforming the world, but I was interested in transforming my world. If I was involved in community, it was because it served a self-centered purpose. Either it linked to my children's activities, or it gave me an opportunity to expand my business network. I coached cheerleading, assisted my husband with running little league football, and opened my home when necessary to my many nieces and nephews. I would take my children with me to Duquesne University's community service day. We've picked up trash along the Allegheny River, painted and cleaned a home for teenage mothers, and read to the elderly. I was not involved in nonprofit organizations because of their cause but because of their potential to build my resume. I didn't view myself as an example for others; my life was not meant for them to emulate. It was me making sense of a chaotic world and striving to come out on top. I thought I had life figured out. I had no idea of the longer journey that awaited me.

This thought process continued as I transitioned from college to career. I took and passed all five parts of the certified public accountant exam during my senior year of college on my first try. After a series of career moves, I ultimately landed in a Big Four accounting firm. I continued to get promoted until I found myself in the ranks of senior leadership within my practice area. I was actively involved in the community, giving both time and money to address some of the most pressing needs because it was good for me. It made me feel good. I was still quite inward focused and proud of it. I was making it happen. I went from being a fatherless, poor African American girl from a blue-collar community to a middle-income business professional whose star was rising. I wasn't supposed to do these things. Financial security was within my grasp, and the good life I dreamed of for myself and my family was around the corner. That was all that mattered to me. I wasn't looking to solve the world's problems, and I wasn't looking to engage in community beyond giving money to "pay back" some of the investment that had been made in me. That was how I thought it worked, and that was what I thought was the measure of greatness—a good title, good income, and philanthropy. I had bought into the world's definition of greatness and was well rewarded for it. Because of my "success," I was held up by several leaders as a role model who needed to be more engaged in diversity and inclusiveness.

I hadn't set out to be a role model, and I didn't want to be a role model. I had set out to do my work and to make a lot of money doing it. My goal was not to influence people or challenge culture, yet that was exactly what I was doing. I had gained a platform of influence that I hadn't sought out or desired, but it was there just because I had worked hard at being the best that I could be within my chosen profession for pretty self-serving reasons. I didn't pursue my CPA license because I wanted to convince other young black boys or girls that they could become CPAs or excel in other finance and accounting professions. I wasn't looking to make a statement. I pursued it because I was going into the field of accounting and therefore felt it only fitting that I apply myself to excellence, and that meant getting the CPA. However, because I did obtain the CPA, I was now a role model.

That realization scared me because I was suddenly made aware of others, and I was suddenly expected to look out for them (even if for political and business reasons) and not just focus on myself. My self-centered focus began to show itself for what it was. As I started engaging with others (again for self-serving reasons), I began to realize that the greatness I thought I had achieved was fleeting and shallow. It was based on all the wrong things. It was based on my accomplishments as marked by pedigree, titles, and awards. The façade was beginning to be stripped away. I had to ask the question as to why my life values did not include or consider other people. I began to think about what legacy I was truly establishing, and I didn't like the answers. I had become quite self-indulgent as pretty expensive wants became needs. I didn't just want that higher-end name brand purse—I had to have it. I needed the club membership, the spa membership, and regular theater nights accompanied by dinner at a higher-end restaurant. The more I looked within, the more I realized that I had to change.

I knew that there was a better version of me than what the world was experiencing. I had to face the fact that I had become a version of myself that was not very attractive, though it was great by the world's standards. The thought of stepping out of my own way to achieve a greatness that mattered terrified me. It sounds easy, but it's not as easy as it sounds. My identity had begun to get wrapped up in this high-income, suburban executive lifestyle. I understood that there was a different definition of greatness but still hadn't yet fully grasped its form.

Here's the funny thing about this realization: the same selfishness that fueled my career began to fuel my doing good. I dug into the D&I and became a mentor, speaker, and advocate for many. I got even more involved in charity and worked diligently to be a good community steward. I did a lot of good for a lot of people, but it was still for the wrong reasons. I gave everything I had to give and then some. I overcommitted myself and then drove myself to a point of burnout. I was determined to obtain as much of a reputation for doing good as I had gained as a business leader. I was now operating at 100 percent on two fronts. Some of my good intentions were not materialized because I failed to recognize and operate within my physical, emotional, and financial boundaries. I learned that I cared about a lot of different things, and so there was a lot of good in my heart. However, I mistakenly believed that I needed to be involved in all of them—that was ego talking. Because of my self-focus, even while doing good, I became a liability instead of an asset. However, I didn't want to let anything go because of my reputation. How would that have looked if I walked away from a charity?

Instead of humbling myself and admitting that I couldn't do it all, some of my promises went unfulfilled. I had to cancel out of activities, some personal and some social, with very little notice. I failed to perform tasks that had been assigned to me by the requested timeline because I was the savior coming to the rescue of all those in need. In my desire to be great, to chase after it with everything I had, I ceased to be effective.

When I realized this, I began to study great organizations to see how they managed themselves. I noticed that these organizations, whether for profit or not-for-profit, limit their focus to no more than three areas because they recognize that they can only spread their resources so far. They know their core competencies, and they exploit those core competencies to their full potential. Instead of trying to do many things well, they focus on doing a few things with excellence. I decided that if I could just do that, greatness was mine. All I had to do was learn to exhibit that same level of discipline and focus in my own greatness quest. I now had a model to follow. I still thought greatness was something I needed to achieve by what I did. I still didn't understand its true form, but I was getting closer. My desire to focus led me into a period of introspection. And that's when God began to speak to me.

Only through spending time in quiet contemplation did I begin to understand that my true purpose in life was to be and not to do. Though I possessed many talents, there's was only one overriding purpose that defined my calling. There was a person I was to become, and if I was to become that person, I would have to walk away from all that "I" had built up. I was going to have to walk away from the title, the income, and the influence I had worked so hard to achieve so that I could actually learn to be me. Now, I don't believe that's true for every person, but it was true for me. I don't believe that all people will have to leave their jobs or vocations as part of their path to greatness, but I did. For some people, the work that God needs to do in you to mold you into who you are to be can happen right where you're at. However, regardless of what path lies ahead of you, what will always be true is that your journey toward greatness really won't begin until you stop trying to achieve and begin allowing God to begin to mold you into what you were uniquely created to be. In that sense, your challenge will be the same as mine. You'll be challenged to die to yourself because that is the very essence of greatness.

Greatness comes from a return to our true nature—people made in the image of God. Doing so comes through separation from what we believed we needed to have and do to achieve self-actualization. Although all will be asked to die to self, their realization of that dying will look different than anyone else's realization based on each person's uniqueness. Therefore we must be careful not to sabotage ourselves as we go on this journey by engaging in comparison. Though I will talk about my life within this book in order to illustrate the process, it's the concepts that are important and not the specific manner in which those concepts were applied to my life. God desires to be as unique with you in forming your character as He is in forming you; allow Him that flexibility. Our society wires us to compare ourselves to others to assess our looks and evaluate our level of success. We judge our quality of life not based on how well we are living out our purpose and enjoying the world that God has provided to us, but rather by how much we have compared to others. Our ambition becomes selfishly focused instead of being righteously focused on others. We cease looking to make others greater than ourselves and turn our attention toward making our names great. We're only happy if we're out front and visible, even when (or especially when) serving. Behind-the-scenes service doesn't satisfy us because we don't get the recognition we desire. If we're truly to achieve what we're meant to achieve in life, we have to move beyond needing the accolades, adoration, and approval of people. It shouldn't matter to us whether our child goes to a local community college or to an Ivy League school as long as they're where they supposed to be based on their God-given purpose in life. It shouldn't matter whether our neighbors drive a Lexus while we drive a used Ford as long as we're living out our purpose. It shouldn't matter whether you're surrounded by women carrying designer purses while you're sporting a spiffy thirty-dollar purse from your favorite department store as long as you're focused right where you're supposed to be focused. And if you happen to have any of those luxuries mentioned, enjoy them as long as you're living out your God-given purpose. Greatness is not to be measured in the things we have or don't have; rather, it's measured based on whether we're living true to who we were designed to be. It's about whether our values are properly aligned, whether our attitudes and behaviors are fitting, and whether the work we do is what was intended for us to do. Doing what we were meant to do with the time and resources we've been given is all encompassing. That result can only be achieved if we submit ourselves to something (someone) greater. This is what is meant by dying to self. Our character develops as we die. As we recognize what truly matters and let go of all the world's false promises, we begin to step into what we're truly meant to be. Greatness is the end result; it's the by-product.

Now that you know what greatness is and is not, what reasons are there for you to want to pursue this type of greatness and step away from the rat race of modern culture?

CHAPTER 2

WHY SHOULD I ASPIRE TO BE GREAT?

Within each of us lies a desire to be significant. This desire was instilled in us as a part of our design. As such, it is not a desire that we can or should ignore. It is not evil or wrong or immoral. However, it can lead to evil, wrong, or immoral behavior when it's distorted and misdirected. The search for significance can lead to tyrannical domination of other people, manipulation of people's good nature and loving hearts, and an obsessive self-centeredness. When we look upon the collateral damage associated with people's unending quest for significance, it can sour us toward having greatness as a goal. We need to avoid falling into that trap at all costs.

What children do you know who aspire to be on the losing team? They want to win. Athletes that have ever won medals did so because they aspired to win. They didn't go into the competition hoping to just finish the course—they wanted to dominate. They may have even wanted to set a new world record. Aspiring to greatness motivates us. We work harder and study harder. We are more disciplined with our time, resources, and decisions. If you take away that motivation factor, you've taken away a key source of passion and commitment and drive. This is one of several reasons that I'm not a fan of participation trophies and ribbons that are handed out for just showing up. We're not meant to just show up; we're meant to push ourselves, to develop our abilities, and to flow in our gifts. But if doing so makes no difference in the outcome, then what is our motivation to do the hard work required to get better? Sure, we could just do it based on our own sense of integrity and our own commitment to excellence, but we're not wired that way. We weren't designed to do things half-heartedly. Man is the apex of creation. We had a mandate: we were to rule.

We're designed as social beings with a need to connect into social groups that allow us to contribute. If we can just show up and do nothing, then our contributions don't matter and the social group ceases to matter. Nothing about that fact has changed as society has changed. We are wired to achieve, to make a difference, to matter. When we stop believing that it's possible for us to achieve this goal, we settle and become complacent. We begin to just check in and go through the motions of life without much purpose or direction. We think it has to be that way, but that's a lie. It doesn't have to be that way. We do not have to settle for a life of punching the clock, earning a paycheck, and hoping the years roll by. We don't have to "wait" to be noticed as high potential or a rising star. We don't have to walk in mediocrity.

I don't have many pet peeves, however near the top of my list are people who make others feel as if they don't have what it takes to be great, that they are lacking in potential and not worth the investment of time or energy. This tells me that the person either hasn't yet grasped the realities of what truly makes us tick as human beings or doesn't care enough about people to see beyond the surface. Most talents ("gifts") do not come wrapped in a package with a nice big bow on them. You have to dig for them. You have to search beneath the exterior and then call out what you see. You have to speak into being the greatness that actually lies within each person. For you to want to do that, you first have to believe that inner greatness does truly exist.

One of my greatest challenges as a coach is getting people to see that they possess greatness. It's not something that they have to develop; rather, it is something that they have to get into the right position in order to unleash. I don't believe that any person is destined to be average or mediocre. People aren't meant to settle for what life has dealt them. Every one of us is perfectly designed for greatness. We are designed to have great relationships:

- with God
- with our spouse
- with our fellow man
- within a community
- within the church

Each relationship meets a different aspect of our desire for significance. Our challenge is to understand the intended role of each one and to order our lives accordingly. When we fail to do that, we begin to substitute counterfeit measures of greatness. This is when our natural drive for significance becomes distorted and misdirected. If not corrected, we can engage in behaviors that inflict significant harm on ourselves and others. Yet it doesn't change the fact that we were designed for greatness and bestowed with incredible gifts by our creator. It simply means that we are offtrack.

There was a time that I aspired to win achievement awards, have my name listing among the who's who of most powerful black women, be featured in the top black magazines, and get featured on *Oprah*. For me, that was the epitome of greatness. I envisioned myself jetsetting around the world and speaking to large groups of people about my motivational journey. I would donate a portion of my fortune to charity to help those less fortunate, and of course I'd be handsomely applauded for having done such noble work. My name was going to be known, and I was going to have all the rewards that go along with fame. In just this one short paragraph, I captured four substitutes for greatness that are common in our culture: achievement, fame, philanthropy, and fortune.

1. Achievement. We live in an achievement-enamored society. We have awards for everything—most influential, most powerful, rising stars, and more. The entertainment world has Oscars, Grammys, Emmys, Espys, and more. Authors aspire to be at the top of the best-seller lists. Salespersons aspire to be the top seller of the year. In this type of culture, it's almost impossible to not equate achieving top billing with greatness. Yet we must resist this temptation. Achieving an award measures a specific outcome. Only one person can win the coveted award even if all pursue that award with excellence, causing the performance of all to improve. Yet there's nothing about winning the award that signals character. You can be an Oscar winner and not have a character profile that is to be admired. Achievements do not equate to greatness.

2. Fame. Our American culture idolizes famous people. Their every move is chronicled. Their clothing choices and food choices are analyzed and imitated. Their relationships are followed with a fanatical obsession. Is it any wonder that fame can become an enticing substitute to greatness? Why seek true greatness where you may labor in obscurity when you can chase fame and be worshipped? Why invest hours in mentoring and coaching on a one-on-one basis when you can have millions of people hanging on your every word? As intoxicating as fame may be, it is not a meaningful substitute for true greatness.

3. Philanthropy. We have a tendency to lavish extravagant praise onto those that make large charitable donations or launch significant social projects with private capital. We like big and splashy. And it's not that big and splashy can't get work done or generate results. It's just that big and splashy tends to shift the focus from celebrating the good work that is being done onto the person funding the work. There's a lot of great work that is done by individuals whose names will never be known. There

are millions of people that may only be able to donate five or ten dollars, but if ten million people donate five dollars, you have fifty million to work with, and if those ten million donate ten dollars, you'd have one hundred million. Great things can be accomplished by people who have little as it relates to resources if they are willing to act in a unified manner. Greatness doesn't require a material treasure trove; it simply requires is a willing heart committed to using all that it has at its disposal to do good toward all those that are within its range of influence.

4. Fortune. Don't misunderstand me here; I'm not against wealth. I do not believe that poverty is a requirement of greatness. I don't believe that owning quality material possessions is evil, wrong, or lacking in compassion. I do believe that there should be rewards for hard work and that we should enjoy the blessings that have been so generously lavished upon us by our Creator. The Earth is a beautiful place, and I have no problem with those who enjoy exploring it through travel. In fact, I hope to be able to do more exploration during this season of my life. So when I talk about fortune becoming a substitute for true greatness, what I'm really talking about is fortune becomes that thing we aspire to as a measure of our success and worth. Fortune doesn't equate to character. We shouldn't look at someone who has a fortune as someone to be emulated and modeled. Fortune can be acquired without being a person of integrity. Fortune can be acquired without being a person who respects, cares, encourages, supports, and loves others. Fortune can be acquired without treating other people with dignity, empathy, mercy, grace, and forgiveness. Fortune can be acquired without being a person who values kindness, truth, and patience. However, greatness cannot be achieved without being a person of character who treats people respectfully and lovingly.

God desires us to experience greatness and to know good things. We should want to have a good name and a good reputation, and we should want to do good works. Having that aspiration isn't wrong; it's at the very heart of our creation. We were made for greatness. We were designed to be in meaningful, enriching relationships. We were fashioned for greatness. We're creative beings. We're meant to create great works. We're imaginative beings. We were meant to imagine great things. We're adventurous beings. We're meant to go on great adventures and make great discoveries. Greatness is a worthy goal. But before we can obtain it, we must recognize that greatness is not a matter of achievement, fame, philanthropy, or fortune. Rather, it is reflected in the quality of our relationships. How could we change our world if we grabbed hold of that realization? What would happen if we all aspired to have great relationships where we sought after the good of others? What if we committed to serve one another with love and kindness? How might that focus change our homes, our schools, our communities, our churches, and our workplaces? Judgmental and critical natures, and the havoc they wreak, would cease to exist. Imagine if you spoke words of correction and discipline with love. If people knew you had their best interests at heart when you provided feedback, how might their reactions change? If people knew that you wanted them to prosper and succeed, how much more open might they be with you? Imagine a community where no one had to worry about someone else trying to take advantage of them to get ahead. The anger, discord, and hatred that mar our communities would disappear.

The answer to what plagues us is so simple, yet it is not easy. If you desire to see peace in your homes, aspire to greatness. If you aspire to see a healthy, productive culture in your workplace or within society, aspire to greatness. If your desire is to see the church grow, aspire to greatness. Die to self and begin to serve others. Stop asserting your rights and yield. Love those who hate you just as much as you love those who love you. Do what's right not because it will benefit you but because it is right. Help those who need help even if they can't return the favor, even if it costs you. Stop calculating the return on investment of every word spoken or every minute spent talking to a friend, a coworker, or a family member. Is greatness desirable? Absolutely! We weren't destined for a life of mediocrity. Yes, we should desire greatness. It's at the very heart of who we are. But is greatness achievable? Absolutely, but doing so will cost you everything.

CHAPTER 3

IS GREATNESS REALLY ACHIEVABLE?

In the Bible, Joseph was sold into slavery by his jealous brothers and jailed for a crime that he didn't commit. There's nothing about his early life that would suggest that he would rise to prominence in Egypt, save his family from starvation, and ultimately become second only to Pharaoh. Moses was given up by his parents to save his life, was raised as a foster child, and became a fugitive from the very ones who had reared him. On top of that, he had a speech impediment. There's nothing within Moses's profile that would suggest that he could lead the Jewish people out of bondage and knit them into a nation. David was a young shepherd who spent his time out in the fields living with the animals he tended until being called into his home to be anointed as the future king of Israel. He had done nothing of note at that time. He hadn't yet slayed Goliath, and he hadn't yet been called into the king's service. There was no visible sign of greatness in Joseph, Moses, or David, yet these men all became great heroes within Israel's history.

Jesus had not yet faced the temptation in the wilderness, and neither had he healed any sick or delivered his famous Sermon on the Mount when God indicated that "this was His son in whom He was well pleased." Peter was identified as a pillar of the yet-to-be birthed Christian faith despite knowing that he was going to deny Christ three time and desert the life of a disciple to go back to fishing. Saul was one of the greatest persecutors of Christians when he was called to bear witness to the gospel. He was on his way to drag Christians out of their homes and to their deaths when he had the encounter that would radically change his future. Great destinies were spoken over Jesus, Peter, and Paul before they materialized. There was nothing that these men had done at the time the declarations were made that would suggest that they would change history, yet change history they did. Regardless of where you stand currently as it relates to the Christian faith, you cannot deny its indelible effects on human history.

David Wilkerson was serving as a pastor in the small rural town of Philipsburg, Pennsylvania, when he was moved by an article to go to New York to help teens on trial for murder. He barely had enough money to get to the city. Thus began the humble beginnings of a street ministry from which Teen Challenge would emerge. Teen Challenge has gone on to serve thousands of men, women, boys, and girls worldwide who face life-controlling problems. Life transformations are occurring simply because one man dared to get involved. Or consider the Donaldson family. Who would think that the tragic loss of a father at the hands of a drunk driver would plant the seeds for what would become Convoy of Hope, one of the premiere outreaches to those who are impoverished, hungry, and hurting? More than 79 million people have been served throughout the world by Convoy of Hope. Convoy of Hope is often first on the scene when disaster strikes to provide comfort and relief to those most in need. Life transformation is happening simply because a man committed to meeting a need. Who would think that a dream in the heart of one young lady would result in a children's home that now spans sixty-five acres? But that's exactly what has happened with Compact Hillcrest Children's home in Hot Springs, Arkansas. There are so many other stories that I could highlight of men and women, young and old, wealthy and poor, educated and uneducated, and from many ethnic backgrounds accomplishing the seemingly impossible simply because they were willing to fully surrender themselves and submit themselves to the process by which true greatness is achieved.

You only need to look back in history to see that greatness is absolutely achievable. We see that with William Wilberforce, Mother Teresa, Nelson Mandela, and Mahatma Gandhi, and we celebrate it. Is it common? No, but it also isn't rare, and it could easily become common if we made the process to achieving it less mysterious. It's important that we settle this fact in our minds and in our hearts because goals that we believe are beyond our reach are demotivating. Why put in the time and effort to live a disciplined and intentional life if you're guaranteed to fail? If you've ever had a subject that you couldn't grasp no matter how much time or energy you put into it, then you understand the build-up of frustration that eventually leads to checking out of the process. I didn't struggle with academics; whether it was math, science, languages, history, or psychology, I could master it if I put my mind to it. Video gaming, however, is another story. I couldn't manage to execute the precise series of buttons I have to push to initiate particular moves if my life depended on it. I look at the ease with which expert gamers fight with their characters with fascination and awe. Their movements are fluid. They switch modes with ease. They look with anticipation on that which I would look on with dread. Imagine if not only was I tasked with becoming a gaming expert, but if my very livelihood was dependent on achieving this goal. How long do you think it would take for me to throw my hands up, walk away discouraged, and believe that my future was hopeless? Unachievable goals will suck the very life out of you.

Fortunately, greatness doesn't fit that bill. Instead of sucking the life out of you, it will energize you. Much like exercise, it will hurt initially but then that breakthrough happens. You begin to see a change in how you think, how you relate to other people, and what motivates you. Those changes fuel you to keep going. Then you're different. You no longer have to work at thinking a certain way; it has become a part of you. You no longer have to work at seeing people's hurts and needs. You can't help but see it because you're so attuned to other people. It's become as natural as breathing, and you can't help but to act. To not act when it's within your power to do so becomes unfathomable to you. Others will begin to ask you how you do all that you do, and you really can't answer that question because you're simply being you. Yes, it's hard work. Yes, you get tired. Yes, you get frustrated at times. Yes, you need rest and sometimes pull away from it all. But in the end, you keep going because what else would you do?

Yes, greatness is demanding. There's no doubt about that. It's a simple life but not an easy one. It will demand all your heart, soul, and strength for the rest of your life. You don't retire from a life of greatness. You may change vocation, but you still have a purpose to serve. It will challenge you to give your all, to leave nothing on the table. The good news is that you don't have to worry about getting bored or lacking motivation because the goal is too easy to achieve. The goal will grow you because you will have to invest all your time or energy into it. This is not a guaranteed lay-up, and so there is no excuse for lower your performance output, checking out and becoming disengaged, or opting up. In the workplace, when we have a high performer who's told to slow down so that others don't look bad, we've just taken the wind out of the person's sails. It's only a matter of time before the person checks out and disengages. The development process has been arrested. Fortunately, greatness doesn't do that. It doesn't tell you to back off. It expects 100 percent sweat equity. Sure, you might have to patiently wait for the right timing to take certain actions, but even then you're not idle. You're going through a preparation process that often involves studying, learning new skills, meeting new people, and gaining new insights about the world. You're working hard but in a different way. The road to greatness is not an easy road, but it's not an impossible road. You will not get bored. It will take time to get there. You will have to trust the process and not try to jump ahead before it's time. Sometimes that is hard. We can be impatient beings; we even put names on our impatience. We say that we're driven, action-oriented, initiative takers when really we just want to be in the driver's seat. Our egos want control, and waiting runs counter to our egocentric nature. As tempting as it may be to skip a particular step, you must resist that urge. You also must resist the urge to accept the norm. Your personality style isn't an excuse. You must look beyond your circumstances and stop giving yourself excuses for opting out of the process. Your socioeconomic status doesn't prevent you from greatness. Your age doesn't prevent you from greatness. Your talents and abilities doesn't prevent you from greatness. Let's look at each of these excuses in turn.

I'M TOO RICH, POOR, UNEDUCATED, WHATEVER ...

Because greatness is not dependent on your social or economic status or on your demographic profile, your environment is irrelevant. It doesn't matter whether you were born poor or rich. It doesn't matter whether you were born into a single-parent home or a two-parent home. It doesn't matter whether you family wrote the book on dysfunction or would be the poster ad for family of the year. It doesn't matter whether you received a top-notch education, never graduated high-school, or received your GED as an adult. All of the metrics that we often use as indicators of personal success are irrelevant when it comes to greatness. That also means that there are no excuses. You can't blame your parents, your teachers, your coaches, or your family members for your failure to achieve greatness. Greatness is 100 percent dependent on the decisions that you make. Certainly, your environment may create interference such that some of those decisions are more difficult to make. The environment may create obstacles so that you have to worker harder than others to grab hold of greatness. But your environment doesn't prevent you from achieving greatness.

I know men and women who have endured unfathomable sexual abuse and whose character is beyond reproach. They could use their background as an excuse to inflict harm on others and go through life bitter, angry, and untrusting, but instead they have chosen to pursue healing and wholeness so that they can speak life into others who have endured similar circumstances. I have also seen the excuse of urban poverty thrown out as the reason for urban crime. Under this theory, individuals have no choice but to succumb to the allure of street life and easy drug money because their options are limited; in essence, they're a victim of their environment. But the reality is that these individuals have chosen to allow their environment to define who they are and have chosen to become instruments of darkness instead of choosing to be sources of light. They choose to become a plight to their community. Admittedly, other paths may not be easy to walk. They may come at great risk to individuals and their families. It may seem unfair to ask individuals to pay that price to break away from an environment that they were placed into by circumstances beyond their control. But isn't that exactly what greatness does? Greatness rises above. It looks not toward what was or even what is, but it looks toward what could be, and it moves accordingly. It refuses to accept the chains that the environment would like to place upon it but rather sees the freedom that awaits ahead if, but only if, a different path is chosen. I often call this "The Road Less Taken," which is what I always called the poem written by Robert Frost, one of my favorite poets when I was a teenager. The poem is actually called "The Road Not Taken," but I always think of it in terms of its final sentence: "Two roads diverged in a wood, and I—I took the one less traveled by, and that has made all the difference."

Those who rise above their environment take the road less traveled, and they make the unpopular decision. That is one of the reasons they are able to achieve greatness.

I'M TOO YOUNG, OLD, WHATEVER ...

You don't have to reach a certain age to obtain greatness; it is available to young and old alike. The wisdom that leads to greatness awaits all that seeks it out. We can call out people like Moses, who was eighty years old when he led Israel out of Egypt and continued to lead them for another forty years as they lived in the wilderness learning how to be the people of God they were called to be. But we can also call out people like the prophet Samuel and Joan of Arc. Samuel was called by God to be a prophet to the nation of Israel as a young boy. Joan of Arc, a daughter of a farmer, was a teenager when she rose up and led the French army to important victories during the Hundred Years' War. She lived in a time when women did not lead. Her methods would've been considered unconventional at the time, and that's very common as it relates to greatness. You will often be labeled as eccentric or radical or confrontational. You may not be popular; challenging the status quo is hardly ever popular, and you have to be comfortable with that reality. Joan of Arc certainly was comfortable with standing out from the crowd.

Fast-forward to more modern times, and we can see the same dynamic still at work. Fawzi Koofi, an Afghan politician and women's rights activist serving as a member in Afghan's Parliament, was twenty-five or twenty-six when she began her political campaign. Fawzi was nineteenth out of her father's twenty-three children by his seven wives and was the last of her mother's children. Her circumstances could have held her back because she lived in a country that oppressed women and did not believe in educating girls. Her age could have held her back. What in the world does a young women in her twenties know about politics or changing the culture of not just a nation but an entire belief system? Do you think Fawzi faced opposition? Do you think her choices were popular? Do you think that fame and fortune has chased her down and lined her pockets? Fawzi certainly has positioned herself to positively influence her environment at great expense to herself. Only history will show what the ultimate outcome is. That's one of the challenges of greatness: final outcomes may be decades or generations into the future, and you may not see them. However, we can certainly applaud her for being willing to take up a fight that many haven't been willing to take.

Moving a little closer to home, Elise Stefanik was only thirty when she was elected to Congress in a landslide victory. It's still far too early to determine the content of her character, to say what influence she will have, or to evaluate whether she'll use her platform appropriately. However, the courage that she's displayed in putting herself out front to lead is commendable. That type of courage can be used to accomplish great things. She certainly has the potential for greatness, and early indications suggest that she's on that path even if we can't yet see how well she will finish her race.

Lest we believe that there's ever a time when you can check out of the process, let's turn our sights to those who started on their path to greatness later in life. We already saw that Moses was eighty years old, but what about Laura Ingalls Wilder, Colonel Sanders, Grandma Moses, or Abraham? Laura was sixty-five years old when *Little House in the Big Woods* was published, and she was seventy-six when the last book in the *Little House on the Prairie* series was released. Her gift for writing had always been there, but it lay dormant for many years as she tended to family. Though she was sixty-five, she had not yet come into her full purpose for being. Colonel Sanders began the Kentucky Fried Chicken franchise when he was sixty-five. His business aptitude was always there, but the right opportunity hadn't come along, and the other aspects of his character still had to be developed before he was ready. It took a while, but eventually all came together and KFC was born. Grandma Moses began painting at the age of seventy-six, worked for twenty-five more years, and produced one thousand works of art. The artist in Grandma Moses was born at seventy-six; it had always been there, but the opportunity to give expression to that person didn't emerge until the later years of her life. Abraham was seventy-five when he set out for Canaan, the land of promise, and Sarah was sixty-five. Today, because of the difference in lifespans, it's best to think of this as Abraham started his journey at fifty. That is a long time to wait to "begin" stepping into your purpose. Who leaves the comfort of home and family to go to an unfamiliar land for an unknown purpose in the "waning" years of their life—and then spends another twenty-five years waiting for the promise to come true? Yet Abraham was on a quest for something greater than himself. He understood that there was a greater purpose to be served, and he was committed to serving that purpose. Like many of the leaders explored in the introduction, Abraham wouldn't see the fruit of what he began. Yet his faithfulness continues to speak to us today.

As you can see by these examples, age doesn't qualify us for greatness, and it doesn't disqualify us. We can't blame our environment, and we can't blame our age. But we're not done yet because as humans, we're great with coming up with excuses and blame shifting. To make sure we've covered all of our bases, we will look at one other factor that has no bearing on achieving greatness: our own abilities.

I'M NOT A GREAT ATHLETE, SINGER, COMPUTER NERD, OR WHATEVER ...

You don't have to possess a particular giftedness to be great. I know grocery clerks, cooks, janitors, teachers, lawyers, politicians, musicians, artists, athletes, stay-at-home moms, truckers, construction workers, graphic designers, and pastors who are steadfastly walking their paths toward greatness. They get up each day seeking to serve others using their particular gifts. They are passionate about what they do and seek to do it with excellence. They take responsibility for their actions and for the consequences of those actions. They have grabbed hold of the notion that life is about something greater than wealth or experience accumulation. As they go about their day, they interact with people in a way that reflects the person's intrinsic value. Their hellos are not reserved just for those individuals capable of doing something for them. These are the people whom you love to serve, work with, and hang around because you see the joy shine through as they give of themselves.

Can you be that type of person? Absolutely. You don't need to be a master of your craft to be great. You simply have to use the talents and abilities that you possess in an appropriate manner. You have to see your job as more than just a paycheck; it's a vocational calling. You have to see service as more than a good thing to do; it's a mission. Taking care of your home and you family is more than just fulfilling obligations; it's ground-zero ministry. Treating workers fairly isn't just great for business; it's a moral imperative. Honoring your commitments isn't about quid pro quo but staying in right relationship with people. Being kind to your neighbor isn't done just to make your life easier; it is also done to show the love and compassion in your heart. You focus your attention on what you can do with the abilities you have instead of what you can't do. Are you able to write and have a message that would encourage and inspire people? Then blog, write an article, or publish a book; offer to share another person's story who doesn't have the gift of writing. Just do something. Are you able to cook? Then cook a meal or two at a family center, homeless shelter, community day, or street block party. Just do something. When a challenge presents itself, look at it as an opportunity to grow. Instead of focusing on what you can't do or the resources you don't have, engage your imagination to think about what you could do with what you do have. Look for opportunities to learn more so that you have even more abilities to bring to the table. There are things you'll never be able to do until you jump in and do them. How did I learn to start a business? I started one. How did I learn to write a book? I wrote one. How did I learn to speak publicly? I accepted public speaking engagements. Yes, I did my homework before taking each of those steps, but eventually I had to take the plunge.

How did I grow in compassion? I began spending time with people in need. How did I grow in patience? I walked through difficult life circumstances (my own and others). How did I grow in forgiveness? I allowed myself to be vulnerable around people. How did I grow in mercy? I listened to people's stories and allowed myself to feel their pain. Yes, I read widely on coaching, counseling, behavioral psychology, and the like. But all the reading is the world is pointless if I'm not out interacting with people. Character building doesn't happen because you read a book. Character building happens because you get into the trenches of life with people. Books help to inform, but experience helps to shape. If you really want to develop your own character and accomplish something that will have a positive influence on the world, you're going to have to take chances. You will have to step outside of your comfort zone. You will have to enter into the unknown.

Greatness is absolutely achievable, but only if we are intentionally persistent. First, we have to adjust our thinking. We have to move beyond seeing greatness as something that you acquire through performance and realize that greatness is something that you become. Anyone can become kind, loving, peaceable, patient, joyful, gentle, merciful, compassionate, diligent, faithful, trustworthy, thoughtful, creative, and innovative. You don't need a degree to develop a great character.

The true question isn't whether greatness is achievable. The true question is whether you're willing to go through the process. Are you willing to confront errors in your thinking and then commit yourself to doing the hard work of inner transformation? Are you willing to set aside long-held beliefs, confront some hard truths, and steer yourself down a different path? Every single one of us was created to manifest the glory of God. That means that every one of us was meant to be powerful beyond measure. We were meant to be brilliant, talented, and fabulous. We were all meant to create and innovate and grow. We all possess an inner desire to create. There is an artist that resides in every one of us; whether it's with music, words, dance, paints, technology, or ideas, we all create in some way. There's a reason that scrapbooking is popular despite the fact that one could simply store the photos online at no cost. There's a reason that quilting is popular despite the fact that one can buy quilts for cheaper than for what one can make them. Why do people devote thousands of hours to perfecting their ability to work with ice or sand or wood, other than the fact that we are natural designers? It's in our blood.

We were all meant to soar to new heights in our intelligence and understanding of the world. Some people will do so more formally by becoming botanists, chemists, geneticists, and medical doctors. Some people will do so by studying sociology, psychology, archeology, anthropology, or linguistics. Still others will do so through literary exploration and analysis, cultural travel, and cultural photography. The means by which we create, innovate, and learn about the world are as varied as the lives that comprise this world, and every one of these expressions is a reflection of our innate greatness.

We were also all meant to have rich, meaningful, and long-lasting relationships. There's a reason why restaurants, taverns, and coffee houses continued to experience robust business even in the midst of economically challenging times. People still wanted to be around other people. Though they were cutting corners financially, they still valued the interaction with their friends and associates enough that they continued to incur the associated expenses. We desire a deep intimacy that cannot be met with technology regardless of how advanced it is. No amount of posting, tweeting, snapchatting, or pinning can replace the feeling of connectedness created by shared experiences. It is within this sharing that relationships flourish. Time spent at the zoo with your family is about much more than observing animals in their natural habitat; it's about spending time together and enjoying the beauty of creation. Entering a 5K walk with a team is far more appealing than entering it alone; the distance that you walk or run is the same, but the experience is different. Relationships matter to us—they matter deeply. It's within relationships that greatness is realized. Relationships challenge us to lay aside our selfishness and become people of love and service. We're challenged to look out for the good of others. We're challenged to become people who are kind, gentle, patient, joyful, and peaceable. The most significant challenge we'll ever face on our path to greatness is our own selves.

We are indeed all destined for greatness. However, we can prevent ourselves from achieving that destiny if we're not intentional about mastering ourselves as we journey through life. There's nothing mysterious about a path to greatness; it's one we're all meant to find and travel. The journey, though, will look different for each person. It will look different because of our unique gifting, our unique family compositions, and our unique experiences. The fact that I was the youngest of seven children and only the second girl meant that I experienced family life differently than my oldest brother, even before the death of my father. I had different challenges to overcome than he did, and so my character developed in a different way. I understood service differently than he would have understood it because I spent time in the kitchen with my mother, helping to cook for my large family. Being a black teenager in America in the eighties was different than being one in the early seventies, and so my older siblings would have had different challenges to overcome in the shaping of their character. Going to a predominantly white university and majoring in a subject where I was the only black provided me with character-forming opportunities that were different than those of some of my friends who went to historically black colleges.

It's these unique paths that make life so fascinating. It's also what makes it so easy to derail ourselves so that our character does not develop the way that it should, and we fail to achieve the greatness that was meant for us to achieve. Before looking at these challenges and how we can derail, we will first examine the general path to greatness.

CHAPTER 4

WHAT IS THE PATH TO GREATNESS?

The path to greatness is a unique personal journey for every person. There is no one universal path upon for the character development that leads to greatness, however there are fundamental truths upon which every journey is built. To explore these fundamental truths, we'll need to address spiritual matters because our quest is fundamentally spiritual in nature. Character is not tangible or physical. Character is the sum of our distinctive mental and moral qualities. We experience someone's character through the actions that it drives, and we often define it as the essence of that person. It goes beyond the minds to touch the souls and the spirit. And if that's the case, then we cannot develop character without dealing with the spiritual. So regardless of where you're currently at spiritually, I encourage you to continue reading. You do not have to believe in the inerrancy of scripture for its truths to still apply. Whether or not you believe in the biblical principles upon which this book is based is irrelevant because truth is not dependent upon your professed belief system. Truth always stands the test of time; it doesn't shift with the winds of culture or the tides of popular opinion. It doesn't become more or less true as you age or as your circumstances change.

Let's use a noncontentious example from science to illustrate this truth about truth. The Earth revolving around the sun in an elliptical orbit as it also rotates on its axis is a truth readily accepted today. However, it wasn't always that way. There was a time when it was believed that the Earth was at the center of the solar system and that the sun, moon, stars, and visible planets revolved around it. The fact that this was believed didn't make it true. It simply meant that our understanding of the universe had not yet come aligned with its actual truths. The same can be said of our most pressing philosophical questions. Questions such as what's the purpose of life and what meaning is there to be found in work are central questions that we must deal with on our journey to greatness because they will define our value system, our value system greatly influences our character, and our character determines the level to which we manifest greatness.

By necessity, the trek toward greatness will cause you to wade in deep philosophical waters. You will have to explore the deepest parts of your heart to uncover your real reason for being. There will be hills to climb and valleys to cross as you grapple with assumptions and beliefs that you long held to be true. You will have to determine whether you're willing to let go of anything that stands in the way of truth, including family values and traditions. You may even find yourself having to separate from friends and family in order to stay on the path marked out for you. The path to greatness is not an easy course to travel. There will be times when you want to quit because you've grown weary and have begun to question whether all the effort is worth it. There will be times when it doesn't seem like much fun because, quite frankly, there are times when it's not. Greatness isn't about whether you're able to post happy emojis at all times. Greatness isn't about whether you're operating from a state of abundance at all times. It's not about landing a coveted title or a position that allows you to boast and brag to your online and offline friends. Greatness is a lifestyle and a mind-set.

I'm not a runner by nature. In fact, I'd rather do anything else other than running. I'd rather clean than run, and I'm not big on cleaning (my husband and children can readily attest to that fact). I'd rather go to the dentist than run, and I really don't like going to the dentist. So imagine my surprise when I felt God nudging me to complete a half marathon. I tried to reason with God. I don't run. I don't like to run. I'm still recovering from a ruptured brain aneurysm. I'm not supposed to be able to walk, and you want me to complete a half marathon. I don't have the energy to complete a half marathon. I don't like the cold. I certainly don't like running in the cold. And did I mention that I don't run? No excuse worked, and so I registered for the 2012 Nationwide Children's Hospital Half Marathon. Then the fun really began. I now had to prepare for it. You know what that meant. It meant getting up early during the week and spending ten to fifteen minutes sitting at the edge of the bed and reminding myself why I was doing this crazy thing. After that, I'd groggily and begrudgingly don jogging clothes and shoes, grab the smartphone and earbuds, and head out the door. I would try to get myself psyched up as I went along. My initial jogs were really walks because I had to build up my endurance and fitness. Month after month, this routine went on—not as consistent as it should've been, but with enough consistency to allow me to finish the race.

The following year, I completed two half marathons. After that third half marathon, I decided that the goal had been accomplished and I could hang up my running shoes. I still didn't think running was fun, and I still don't. However, I learned a lot about myself, perseverance, discipline, and faithfulness. They were lessons that I needed to learn. There were times when I wanted to quit, when I wanted to lie down on the side of the road and call it a day. I pressed on. There were many times when I wondered why in the world I had paid money to torture myself. The miles rolled on. Around the ten-mile mark, my thinking began to change. Suddenly, I started to think that I could do this. The worst part of the journey was behind me. The equivalent of a 5K stood between me and the finish line. I could do a 5K in my sleep. It wasn't that my energy meter had skyrocketed; rather, it was the realization that what seemed impossible was now within my sight, and that gave me the jumpstart I need. I could definitely do this; I could cross the finish line. Me, a brain aneurysm survivor, was going to complete this half marathon. I could get the finisher's medal draped around my neck. The completion time really didn't matter to me. The act of finishing was what mattered. A goal had been set, and its achievement was within reach. Now was the time to dig in and push through.

I don't know whether I'll complete another half marathon in my lifetime, but I know that I'm capable of it. I also know that I can dig in and persevere even when every bone in my body hurts, when my skin is chafed, my hands and feet are swollen, and my energy is waning. And so it is with the path to greatness. There will be times when you have to dig in and persevere. Weariness may have seeped into your mind, body, and soul, but you have to keep going. You may need to rest for a time to restore your strength, but once restored, you have to get back at it. You'll question whether the goal is actually worth it. Rest assured that it is. There will be times when you will wonder whether you have what it takes to finish. Rest assured that you do not on your own, but that's where faith and community comes in. So where do you begin?

STEP 1: SEEK WISDOM

The path to greatness begins with acquiring wisdom. Character cannot develop until it is connected to wisdom. Conventional sources define wisdom as the sound application of experience, knowledge, and good judgment. This implies that wisdom is something that you do versus something that you acquire. Under the conventional definition, wisdom is learned over time, which means that it could rarely belong to the young, the uneducated, or the developmentally challenged. The gray-haired old man would be viewed as wise by virtue of time. However, holding to this definition and its resulting view is very short-sighted. If I accumulate forty-years of misinformation and misguided thinking, I'm not wise—I'm just old and dangerous because I'm able to lead others astray as I was led astray.

Instead, I would contend that wisdom is the ability to think rightly so that you're able to discern right action. Wisdom is a talent or ability that is given to those that seek it out. It is a gift that every person is able to unwrap from the young to the old, from the uneducated to the highly credentialed scholar, from the developmentally challenged to the Mensa member. Wisdom doesn't discriminate based on social categorizations. If this is true, if wisdom is truly available to all who seek it out, then it behooves us to understand how we seek it out. When I was a child, my favorite games included hide-and-seek, freeze tag, hopscotch, and jacks. Each game had its own rules and style of play. Knowing how to play hopscotch doesn't help me know how to play hide-and-seek. Likewise, knowing how to acquire worldly wisdom doesn't help you acquire true wisdom. Not only is the acquisition process quite different, but it is also often in conflict. Worldly wisdom can make true wisdom seem foolish; it can make it seem too easy. The reality is that you don't work at acquiring true wisdom in the same way that you work to acquire worldly wisdom. True wisdom isn't based on achieving a particular status but rather in connecting with its source. True wisdom emanates from our Creator, and as we seek a relationship with our Creator, we seek out wisdom. Entering into a genuine relationship with God is our first step toward acquiring wisdom, and therefore it's the first step on our journey to greatness. It's a simple step, but it's not always easy, and so often fear gets on the way. We're afraid of what a relationship with God would really mean. We're afraid of what a relationship with God might cost us. We're afraid of what friends, family, or business associates might say if we suddenly sought out this God whom we may have spoken against (perhaps even vehemently). And although all those fears can be overcome, it's not the express purpose of this book. This book is about the path to greatness. I'm not trying to sell you on God. God doesn't need selling; God's Word is able to speak for itself. I'm here to lay out the fundamental truths that must undergird your journey to greatness if you want to be successful in a way that truly matters.

So if seeking the wisdom that only comes from a genuine relationship with God is the first step, what's the second?

STEP 2: IDENTIFY ERRORS IN OUR THINKING

When we enter into a genuine relationship with God, we are not immediately changed. Our thinking doesn't suddenly change. There is a process that we must follow to have our thinking straightened out. Before we can fix our thinking, we need to understand what's wrong with it. We need to understand the lies we've believed and the truth that needs to replace those lies. Until we do so, our value system will be distorted, and if our value system is distorted, then our character will be as well. There are many lies that we could focus on as it relates to becoming truth seekers, but if we maintain our focus on greatness, then the lies that we really need to confront and the truth that we need to replace them with are as follows.

Our past mistakes do not define us or disqualify us. We are to learn from them and use them to help others gain freedom.

Worldly wisdom tells us that we need to hide our past mistakes. We are to seek to overcome them, put them behind us, and never speak of them again. Speaking of these mistakes is risky and could tarnish our image. This approach creates a bondage of shame that traps us in anxiety and defensiveness. We can't allow people to get to close to us, or they might undercover the truth of who we are. We can't operate from a place of vulnerability and transparency because we could get shamed publicly if we do.

If we cannot overcome our mistakes and put them behind us, never to be spoken of again, then we are assigned labels that indicate we're helpless to do anything other than to give in to them and go wherever they take us. We're labeled as addicts or hardened criminals or whatever, and everyone simply waits for behaviors that are consistent with that label. It doesn't matter how many actions occur that are inconsistent with that label; those are just anomalies and not indicative of an actual change. The labels stay affixed to us, thereby creating a bondage of shame that traps us in anxiety and defensiveness.

Worldly wisdom enslaves. We have to work to overcome, to hide from, to move beyond. True wisdom tells us to that we can learn from our mistakes. We should seek to come to terms with those mistakes and be willing to use them as opportunities to speak into the lives of others, as appropriate. We don't have to share all of the details with everyone whom we meet, but we don't have to hide from them either, and because of that we can be vulnerable and authentic with people. We don't have to worry about people finding out about the skeletons in the closet because we've already incorporated those into our stories. We don't have to concern ourselves with our image because that's not the source of our greatness. Instead, we can speak to the power of perseverance, resiliency, and commitment to change. We can motivate and encourage others facing similar situations. True wisdom is freeing.

For the longest time, I was ashamed of being a teenage mother. I wasn't ashamed of my son, just of how young I was when I had him. I didn't want to tell people my age because they could, by default, calculate how old I was when I had Warren. For the record, I was seventeen and a half and had just graduated high school. Yes, that meant I was pregnant during my senior year of high school. Though it came as a surprise to most, it was a foreseeable outcome of an out-of-control, rebellious life. I took my first drink when I was twelve after being raped by a family friend. I got so drunk that I couldn't even navigate our stairs to go to my bedroom. I continued drinking throughout my middle school, high school, and college years. Even though I didn't turn twenty-one, the legal drinking age in Pennsylvania, until my senior year of college, I had no problem securing alcohol or being served at local establishments. I even supplied some of my high school peers with alcohol. Though I didn't understand it at the time, I was at war with myself. Even while I was engaging in all these self-destructive activities, I was also pursuing knowledge because I wanted to have a future. I was a straight-A, National Honor Society student with offers from several colleges to attend on an academic scholarship. I graduated high school with a semester of college credits. I received a top-level score on my SAT. All the while, I was out of control. No one knew what was truly going on inside of me—not even me.

I would go on to attend a top-rated local university, majoring in business and graduating summa cum laude. Because of this "success," I suddenly had a platform to talk to teenage girls. But what could I talk to them about, really? I was far from a role model with all the poor decisions I had made. How could I talk to them about purity, self-control, and good citizenship when I'd failed so miserably? My character was far from being beyond reproach. If I encouraged them to live purely, what type of hypocrite would that make me? The false belief that I had to keep silent because I had made so many wrong decisions almost stopped me from having meaningful dialogue with many at-risk teenage girls. I thought I was disqualified because of the character flaws I had, but as I began to share my story, I realized that people needed to hear it. They needed to understand that although choices do have consequences, they do not have to become your identity. It's humbling to acknowledge your mistakes to the world. It's also freeing. Worldly wisdom seeks to deny you that freedom, and your character suffers because of it.

Our God-given roles do not limit us. They are to be cherished and celebrated.

Worldly wisdom tells us that the roles of men and women in society are in conflict. Men cannot excel without objectifying, oppressing, controlling, and silencing women. Women cannot succeed without debasing, dishonoring, and emasculating men. The battle lines have been drawn. What started out as a battle for equality has morphed into a battle for domination. Debates rage over who makes for better leaders, men or women, instead of focusing on the development of healthy character within both. Money is poured into building the self-esteem of girls while developing an authentic view of manhood within our boys languishes. Mentoring programs for girls do not lack for volunteers while boys are left longing for role models. A male-dominated occupation is a de facto sign of discrimination. There can be no legitimate reason for such a skewing, and so all efforts must be made to address this issue, and anyone who thinks otherwise is obviously antagonistic toward women.

Similarly, worldly wisdom tells us that motherhood is limiting to women and restricts them from providing true value to society. Career women disrespect stay-at-home moms. Stay-at-home moms have wasted their potential, and worse, they've placed themselves in a position of being dependent on a man to provide financially. These stay-at-home moms are put in a position of having to defend their choice instead of having it honored and respected as a valid and valuable contribution. In the process of defending their choice, stay-at-home moms debase career women and accuse them of permanently damaging their children. The battle lines have been drawn.

On the other hand, true wisdom tells us that men and women are created equal but are also created with different roles. Both are designed to lead. Both are designed to create and innovate. Both are designed to use their intelligence to understand their world. Both are designed to nurture and grow relationships. However, their unique genetic makeup and wiring means that they will do so in very different ways, and because of that, they are naturally suited to partner together in different roles. Certain occupations will continue to be male-dominated while other occupations will be female-dominated; there's nothing inherently wrong with that fact. More women will stay at home to take care of their children then men; there's nothing inherently wrong with that fact. More women will alter schedules and work in occupations that allow more flexibility for childrearing than men; there's nothing inherently wrong with that fact.

Embracing our differences means accepting our differing roles and learning how to live in mutual submission to one another. It means supporting and encouraging one another to walk in our unique gifts and callings, whatever they may be and whether or not they conform to our preconceived notions of what equality actually looks like. It doesn't matter whether your son is called to be a construction worker, a nurse, an athlete, or a fashion designer. His greatness is not dependent on his calling but on his walk, on his character. If your daughter decides to be a stay-at-home mom, she has not thrown her life away if she does so with character. If she chooses to work outside the home, she hasn't doomed her children to a life of drugs, sex, and broken relationships if she lives out a life of character. If she decides to pursue a vocation that is traditionally female instead of going into science or mathematics, she hasn't set back the cause of women everywhere, and she hasn't thrown away her opportunity to be great and influence her world. We once again see that worldly wisdom, though promising freedom, actually delivers bondage.

Faith doesn't hinder us as a society. We must integrate faith and values into our work to succeed.

Faith and values cannot be lived out in our private lives alone. That notion, as appealing as it may be to some, is completely fallacious. Every decision you make is based on what you believe to be true. If you believe that the sole purpose for business to exist is to make a profit for shareholders, you will make different decisions than if you believe that the purpose of business is to glorify God through channeling our creative energy into good pursuits that improve the quality of life and establish vibrant, healthy communities. Ironically, embracing the second definition of business isn't in conflict with making profits, and in many instances it can drive greater profits. It's also at the heart of greatness as a business owner and leader. However, you cannot hold to the second definition of business without an infusion of faith and values into your work.

Likewise, if you believe that people are resources to be prudently managed so as to maximize productivity and minimize inefficiencies, you will make different decisions than if you decide that all people should be treated with love, compassion, and empathy because they are God's image bearers, handmade and handcrafted to do good works based on a distinct set of talents and abilities. Regardless of which viewpoint you embrace, you will encounter people situations that you never anticipated. Perhaps an employee will get sick or have a family emergency in the midst of a critical project, or perhaps your primary market is disrupted, causing decreases in sales and a need for less staff. How you respond, however, will be drastically different. When people are a resource to be managed, their performance review and compensation may be impacted because they let the team down, or they may be fired. When people are image bearers, they are provided assistance to master the ups and downs of life and emerge victorious. It's not enough to treat them with dignity; you want to see them succeed. You don't just give them the time they need to deal with their personal situation (as important as that is); you also get personally engaged in it. You go beyond the bare minimum of helping them land on their feet; you invest in their growth. You help them land in places they never thought possible. You tap into your personal network and invest your personal energy to transform a negative into a positive for them. You're not satisfied with them just getting by; you would ideally like to see them better off than before. Though the second response might cost you more in the short term, the long-term payoff is normally greater. Worldly wisdom, promising freedom, once again delivers bondage—this time to the mighty dollar. True wisdom sets you free to invest in people.

Because so much of our thought process occurs without us really thinking about it, we may not even know that these lies are in operation.

When we're unaware, there's little we can do about them. However, once we've been made aware of them, then we have a decision to make: we must decide whether or not to confront them. Choosing to not confront these three lies and instead choosing to continue to believe that we need to hide our mistakes, fight across gender lines, and relegate our faith to the closet will limit your potential for greatness. Your character development will suffer. Choosing to confront these lies will not result in an instantaneous change in your thinking or improvement in character. Changing our thinking is an iterative process. It doesn't happen all at once, and it also doesn't happen in a linear fashion. You may find that you can only share a part of your story because there's still too much pain associated with other parts. As you receive healing in those other areas of pain, you will be able to share more, but that may be years or decades down the road. If you've been in an abusive relationship or a domineering environment, it may take some time to embrace a vision of mutual submission where men and women co-lead. If you were raised in or suffered under a highly legalistic environment where religion was used as a hammer in a highly punitive fashion, it may take some time to embrace a vision of a faith-infused marketplace. Because of the emotional undertones, this step in the process is the most difficult and takes the longest. Fortunately, this step doesn't have to be completed before the other steps can commence. It can (and normally does) happen concurrently. That's why character improves over time and greatness takes so long to achieve.

STEP 3: LET GOD DEFINE OUR PURPOSE

I participated in my first major spelling bee in sixth grade. I didn't know anything about spelling bees, so how did I end up in one? We could say it was chance, or we can say it was the astute eye of a teacher, but I believe there was something greater at work. I didn't win the spelling bee, but I did learn a lot about etymology. I learned to appreciate the amount of cultural history embedded within the words we use. Although not important to a sixth-grader, this appreciation is invaluable to me today. If you examined my course schedule in high school, you'd think it belonged to someone with multiple personalities. The logical and analytical side of me was on full display within trigonometry, probability and statistics, calculus, philosophy, and data programming. My artistic, creative, and expressive side lived for American literature, creative writing, public speaking, and debate. My big-picture and problem-solving side rocked it out in accounting and business leadership. My love of people and culture compelled me to study multiple languages—parlez-vous francais or comprende espanol? College was equally as eclectic and confusing to the external eye. Required business courses were combined with things like classical art appreciation, classical literature, mythology, and a continued studying of languages. In what possible way could this all come together? Fast-forward over twenty-five years and look at me now. I'm a pastor and a business leader focused on marketplace ministries, a component of which includes running a coaching and leadership development business that I founded. Additionally, I'm a learning executive at a CPA association responsible for leading a team that creates and delivers learning to thousands of CPAs within the state of Ohio. And of course, I'm an author, facilitator, and public speaker. I've traveled the world, and in doing so I had to observe basic etiquette and social customs whether in Brazil, Netherlands, Luxembourg, Germany, India, Great Britain, Mexico, or elsewhere. I interact with people of different backgrounds and belief systems on a regular basis. I've had to learn the nuances of Ramadan and Eid-Al-Fitr for my Muslim friends, the dos and don'ts of honoring Sabbath and major holidays such as Yom Kippur for my Jewish comrades, and the ins and outs of observing various life milestones in religious but non-Pentecostal settings such as Catholic and Jehovah Witness weddings. I've learned how to join in celebrating birthdays and coming-of-age traditions that are far removed from my own upbringing such as first birthdays, bat mitzvahs, and quinceaneras. Through all of this, my cultural inquisitiveness has certainly come in handy.

Now, who could have possibly woven all these seemingly unrelated skills, talents, and interests together into a beautiful tapestry except God? Furthermore, who could've taken a young black girl with no exposure to business or corporate America, raised by a widowed mother in a blue-collar and working-class community, and plopped her into the midst of executive leadership in a Big Four accounting firm except God? As I look back over my life, I understand that there was a process at work to get me to where I'm at today. I didn't see the entirety of the process at the time. I couldn't envision my life today. There was nothing within my fifteen- or sixteen-year-old mind-set that could've begun to paint the picture that is my life today. I didn't even know an entrepreneur at that age, so how could I possibly speak about entrepreneurship or business ownership? I didn't know any authors, speakers, or business trainers—how could I even imagine such a vocation? Until I neared my senior year of college, I didn't even know what CPA stood for let, alone what CPAs did, so how could I have aspired to become one? I didn't believe in God, had no use for the Bible, and had no desire for fellowship or anything that smelled of church, so why in the world would I desire to become a pastor? Nothing in my life today is the result of a grand dream that I had when I was young. Rather, it's the result of God faithfully and painstakingly working out His purposes in my life even before I knew Him. But if you'd asked me what I wanted to be when I grew up, I would've given you an answer that went something like this.

> I was going to be a successful business career woman (whatever that meant) with an equally successful husband (also in business), a nice home (or two, including a vacation home in an exotic location), and no kids so that we could travel whenever and wherever we wanted. Not only would we travel the world together, but we would also take in the nightlife while we were home. Our house would be the center of entertainment. We would have several nice cars and be the envy of all.

When I became a single mother right after high school, my dream changed only slightly. The nightlife was replaced by more cultured experiences, but other than that, the dream remained the same. My son would grow up experiencing the world alongside me. He would travel with me and soak in all the different cultures.

If you look closely at that dream, it was all about me. There's nothing in that dream about how I would use my talents to better society. Ironically, as I've allowed God to work out His purposes in my life and develop me, I've become a successful businesswoman with an amazing (and successful) husband who happens to specialize in the culinary arts. Give him ingredients and a kitchen, and he'll whip up a culinary masterpiece. I'm connected into a church community with church leaders who've poured into my life beyond anything that I could've ever imagined. I've been given a platform to speak into people's lives in meaningful and powerful ways. This same platform allows me to give a voice to those without a voice. I've had opportunities to work with people of great faith to address some of the most pressing societal issues. I live in a nice home in a nice neighborhood with incredible neighbors. I have three amazing children, all of whom love to travel and would like nothing more than to travel the world with me. Our house is a place where you can come and experience hospitality and community. It's not overflowing with activity, but it is overflowing with love, joy, and peace. My dream as a teenager couldn't begin to compare with what God actually had in store for me, but I almost missed it. I almost missed it because my "dream" required that I work all the time. I was a workaholic with a capital W. I didn't shut off. I was performance-driven because that was what was going to accomplish my "dream." That was how I was going to realize my "purpose." In my "dream," I had a lifestyle that required constant upkeep and upgrade. Accomplishing my purposes required striving. Accomplishing God's purposes required waiting and resting. It required spending time quiet time with myself and with God. Accomplishing God's purposes required letting go of preconceived notions of what it meant to be a business leader. I had to allow God to define my business plan. I had to allow God to build my resume. I had to allow God to build my network. I had to let God open doors and close doors. God began to set my appointment calendar. God began to set my priorities. God began to guide my financial outlays. Once this began to happen, what seemed like disparate experiences came together to shape my current vocation. I can now look back over journal entries that I wrote ten to fifteen years ago and see their fruition. I couldn't have arranged the circumstances that caused those ideas or thoughts to come to be—that's a work that only God can do, and God wants to do the same for you. If you allow God to work on you so that you become the best version of yourself, the rest will take care of itself. You won't have to pursue greatness; it will be the by-product of the character development work that God does in you.

As previously stated, we're each created in God's image. But why were we created? That's the answer that's found within our unique purpose. Why were you placed in the family in which you were placed, in the order in which you were placed? Being an only child, a middle child, or the youngest of seven children makes a difference in your personality. Why were you given certain skills and not others? Some people are gifted in the arts; they can paint a picture that will stop you in your tracks. Other people can't draw a decent stick figure. That's not by chance—there's a reason for that. Why do you have the preferences that you have? If you love science but hate reading, there's a reason for that. It's not by chance. There's something about the scientific process that resonates with the very core of who you are. So many books have been written about finding your place in life. Often these books are bestsellers, and some of them are pretty good. The best of these books talk about that intersection of talent, passion, and need, and then they take you on a journey to reflect upon your personal experiences and how they reveal your talents and passions. They're partially right: talent and passion are key indicators pointing you toward your destiny, that unique purpose for which you were made. However, sometimes we can misinterpret or fail to see any connection. I now understand that human psychology was an underlying current throughout all of my seemingly disparate interests. I was driven to understand how people think, why we form groups, why we believe what we believe, how we interpret data, how we make sense of the world, and so on. Now that I've highlighted that underlying theme, go back and take a look at the various interests and topics I mentioned and see how they now come together. I can clearly see the connection now, but I couldn't see it then. There's no way I could've steered myself in the right direction.

The other potential issue with focusing on the intersection of talent, passion, and need is that need is subjective. There are things valued by this world that shouldn't be, and there are things that aren't valued by this world that should be. Sometimes you're called to one of those lesser value areas, and you still need to walk in that. In today's society, do we really need another book on personal leadership? I dare you to google leadership books and see how many books are listed. Even if you narrow the search to Christian leadership, you'll still get thousands of books. We could narrow it even further to Christian leadership in the marketplace, and you'll still have more books than the average reader can consume in a lifestyle. So why am I adding to the collection? Why yet another book? I can't answer that question because God hasn't revealed that to me. All I know is that I'm supposed to write this book. I know that because of God's direction throughout the writing of this book. I can safely conclude that it is meeting a need of some type for someone, but that's as far as I can go. Another tricky thing about need is that we can't always see it. You may not know why you're supposed to open a coffee shop in a section of town that has never supported a coffee shop. The business plan may not add up. The need may not be apparent. You need something beyond an explicitly apparent need to direct you. You need God's direction.

Personality assessments and gift assessments are as popular as books when it comes to finding your place. Life coaching is also rising in popularity as people turn to these individuals to help them make sense of their lives. These are great tools, and I highly recommend them; you'll even find a list of tools within the resources section of this book. However, separated from God's direction, they cannot lead you to that right place. As invaluable as my life coaching training has been for me, it's useless if I separate it from listening for God's voice while I'm interacting with an individual whom I'm coaching. Only God can reveal those things deeply rooted in us that are beyond our conscious knowing. That promotion that seems ideal for you and that you worked so hard to position yourself for may pull you away from the duties and responsibilities that fueled you because they tied into your passions and interests. You could find yourself making more money and having greater prestige but also feeling less satisfied with life and less motivated to perform. What sounded good, and is probably good for someone, wasn't actually good for you. Assessments cannot tell you that; only God's direction can highlight that for you.

God's direction is also important for another reason. We all have blind spots that are visible to others and can be spotlighted by them, but we also have blind spots that are not known by others. Performance improvement often comes from addressing visible blind spots, but personal transformation occurs when invisible blind spots are addressed. Coaches, mentors, friends, employers, or anyone who spends time with you on a regular basis can point out your visible blind spots without needing to tap into God's direction. However, spotlighting those invisible blind spots is something that only God's direction can do. These blind spots may include errors in our thinking that run so deep that they seem to form the core of who we are as a person. Confronting these types of error requires a strength that's beyond us. Only through God's direction are we able to deal with these matters and emerge whole. We must allow God to define our purpose if we want it to be true and unfailing, and then we must make the decision to walk fully in that purpose.

STEP 4: WALK FULLY IN THAT PURPOSE

Walking in your God-defined purpose is a daily challenge. Every day you will have opportunities to make decisions that either propel you forward in that purpose or drag you away from that purpose. As a Christian business leader, I attend numerous networking and team-building events where open bars, coarse joking, and other shenanigans are the norm. It would be easy for me to justify social drinking as the price for doing business and building relationships. It certainly would be easier for me to do that than to constantly have to decline drinks offered to me throughout the evening. I could decide to participate in the coarse joking so as not to stand out or make others feel uncomfortable; I'm sure those I'm networking with would find me much more entertaining if I did. And I can revel in the shenanigans as a way for building memories and deepening relationships with my business associates instead of going back to my room and reading a book. Then I would have stories to share at subsequent conferences or events where these informal networks congregate. I could have a reputation that precedes me and makes people want to hang out with me after hours. However, doing so would drag me away from my God-given purpose. My witness within the marketplace would be tarnished. I must decide to toe the line each and every time. Making the decision once isn't good enough. I have to make that same decision with every event that I attend. And I will need to make that decision every time for the rest of my life. This is a truth that I wish I'd understood when I first entered the marketplace. Because I didn't, I did engage in the social drinking, the coarse joking, and the shenanigans. I was developing quite the reputation as the dancer with a bottomless stomach, able to drink with the best of them. I wasn't walking with God at that time, and it showed. I cringe today when I think about how much I was willing to do to fit in. God doesn't call us to fit in. He calls us to stand out. We're to stand out not because we can drink more than anyone else, or because we're able to tell the funniest stories about our escapades, or because we're able to attract more attention to ourselves. Rather, we're to stand out because of the beauty of our spirits.

You see, when you walk fully in your God-given purpose, you will have peace, order, discipline, and joy. You will be caring and compassionate. You will be creative and innovative. You will be productive and successful in your endeavors. You won't sit around wondering why you were born because you'll know why. You won't need virtual reality to escape because your own life will have meaning. That's not to say that you won't engage in video games—those can be plain old fun at times—but you won't need them to cope with life. You will be the type of person who's talked about because of the results that you attain. People will wander about the secrets of your success. They will want you to be their mentor and coach. They'll want what you have, and sometimes they'll not be thrilled that you have it. That's reality. You'll be able to come to the end of your life without regrets because you lived to the fullest, without retreat and without reserves. You'll know that you held nothing back. That's the type of life we're meant to live—an abundant life.

Living this type of life isn't easy. We're bombarded daily with hundreds of messages of what we need to be happy and satisfied with life. If you truly want to be satisfied, remodel your house so that you can have the bathroom and kitchen you never knew you needed, but now that you see it on television or in magazines, you absolutely must have it now. Or if that won't do it, then take that perfect vacation where you can let your hair down, indulge every whim and fancy, and then leave it all behind when you return to your real life. After all, what happens in Vegas stays in Vegas. And the list goes on. Within all this messaging, what you won't hear is the message that you're purposefully designed by God to fulfill a specific need, and that you won't know true satisfaction until you begin to operate within that role. You will be hard pressed to get advice on how to actually walk in that purpose. Seldom will someone coach you to:

- Turn down a promotion or job offer because it doesn't fit with what you're called to at the moment. Instead, worldly wisdom cloaked within "spiritual" language will be provided to encourage you to go through that open door. After all, if the door is open to you, then it's meant to be.

- Stay the course despite a barrage of challenges, some of which seem insurmountable. Conventional wisdom would advise you to cut your losses and move on to something more productive and less stressful. But if you're walking in God's purposes, you have to stay the course regardless of how impossible it seems.

Because you're not likely to get advice on living a purpose-filled life from contemporary media or your personal network, you need to look to other sources. You need to allow the right voices to speak into your life and quiet the wrong ones. When was the last time you thought about the types of shows you watched, music you listened to, or books you read? Just based on these items, what's being spoken into your life, and does it really match with who you're supposed to be? I've always been an avid reader. In my teen and young adult years, I had what I now can see as an unhealthy fascination with darkness. I loved Edgar Allan Poe, Stephen King, and Dean Koontz. These authors would not be on my top-ten list of authors if you want to nurture a caring, compassionate, and peaceful spirit.

As I advanced in the business world, my attention turned to business books primarily on leadership, negotiation, and sales. Whether it was the *Seven Habits of Highly Effective People* or *Getting to Yes*, I absorbed the principles without question. Never once did I stop to think whether these principles aligned to my core values, or whether they were good and wholesome. They were how the business world worked, and so the rest didn't matter. I allowed these books to define my core values as they related to the business of doing business. In short, I compartmentalized and rationalized. Over the past five years, I've had to unlearn a lot of these principles. I had to begin to filter everything I thought I knew through the lens of who I was created to be within this world. It hasn't been easy. It's amazing how deeply rooted these principles can go. What's wrong with doing first things first or not allowing the urgent to crowd out the important? On the surface, nothing—unless doing so causes you to miss the opportunity to serve people whom you were meant to serve at the time that you were meant to serve them. Sometimes that service happens because you respond to an urgent request. Sometimes that service requires you to set aside your priorities or "first things." There are times when that interrupting knock on the door followed by the often dreaded "Do you have a few minutes?" should command your full attention regardless of the day's schedule. Few leadership books delve into the people side of the business in meaningful ways; life doesn't happen on a schedule. People get sick. Accidents happen. Tragedies strike unannounced. Inevitably, you're made aware of those events by the unexpected phone call or knock on the door. Your response in these moments should extend beyond thinking about employee engagement, loyalty, and profitability. If you're walking in your God-given purpose, there are times when your decision will not align with what's best for the bottom line. There will be other factors you need to consider, and you won't find those factors in your traditional business books.

Unlearning principles is not easy. Thankfully, somewhere along my journey, I rekindled and deepened my study of human behavior. Behavioral psychology books began to grace my shelves along with historical fiction and autobiographies. Imagine my surprise as I realized that as science advances in its understanding of the human brain, it continues to turn traditional understanding on its head and is more aligned with the tenets of faith. The importance of beliefs, values, and purpose are now fully supported by science. Keep in mind that just one hundred years ago, anyone suggesting that people were wired with certain personality traits and abilities would've been dismissed as a quack. Not so today. As much as humans like to rely on science, there's still so much that it doesn't know. Indeed, the body of scientific knowledge continues to grow, and as it does, long-held theories are discarded and new theories emerge. This is just one of many reasons why our truths must be anchored in something other than scientific belief. We must get our counsel from a source anchored in a Godly wisdom that is unchanging and entirely objective. That is the only source that we can truly afford to have speaking into our lives.

Take a close look at your podcasts, books, magazines, television shows, and other sources of advice and ask whether they're a voice that should be speaking into your life. Think about the character that is being developed as you listen to, watch, or read those things. Are they developing the character qualities that you associate with greatness? Are they contributing to you being the best version of you possible, the one that God designed you to be? If not, then you need to discard them for ones that are more wholesome.

Breaking with the unwritten rules of behavior, challenging principles you've learned and held to be true, fixing errors in your thinking, allowing God to define your purpose, and walking in that purpose are simple steps toward greatness, but they are not easy. They become easier tasks whenever you stay focused on your vision. It also helps if you're able to have some idea of what you're likely to encounter along the journey so that you can be better prepared. That's where we'll turn our attention next.

CHAPTER 5

WHAT SHOULD I EXPECT ALONG THE JOURNEY?

The journey to greatness will not be smooth or easy. In fact, at times you will feel like you're in a fiery furnace where the heat has been turned up seven times its normal setting. It's in these defining moments that your character is built. It's a lot like the process used to transform carbon into diamonds. Most everyone loves diamonds, but few people love coal. Yet both are related forms of pressed carbon. Coal is black and dirty. Diamonds are hard, clear, and radiantly brilliant. Coal is pressed carbon that hasn't gone through the same level of pressure as diamonds for the same length of time. Its dark color is the result of impurities still included in it, such as hydrogen, sulfur, mercury, and more. There's a reason coal doesn't smell too great when it's burned. To become that beloved diamond, the carbon must undergo intense pressure over a sustained period of time. Then the greasy luster must be cut away to reveal the shiny brilliance that's underneath. Once the process is complete, a diamond can only be scratched by another diamond. In the same way, we're full of impurities that must be pressed out of us. If we attempt to shine before we've undergone the purification process, our lives will smell about as sweet as burning coal. However, if we allow ourselves to undergo the pressure, we will experience a "molecular" transformation such that our character will become indestructible. We will become brilliantly radiant, drawing attention from near and far because our lives stand out. Our uniqueness will speak for itself as we emit a light that can overcome anything and everything.

For us as individuals, pressure comes in the form of difficult situations and circumstances. You may lose a job unexpectedly. You may be suddenly thrust into the role of caregiver for a sick child or parent. You may suffer through abandonment in the form of infidelity or divorce. The list goes on and on. Persevering during hard times, whatever those hard times might look like for you, will try you at your very core. Not only will there be days when you wonder whether you really have what it takes to endure, but you will also wonder whether you even *want* to endure it. You will question whether it's worth it in the end. It would be easier to give up or give in, especially if you see others having an easy time of it while you're struggling. You may ask why they seem to be enjoying great health when they live so unhealthy, and you, having lived healthy, are battling cancer. Or you may wonder why they seem to be enjoying so many financial blessings while working so little, whereas you work so hard for so little. Or, you might be wondering why their children seem to be doing so well when their parenting skills are lacking while your children are determined to do wrong despite your loving guidance. We become really good at the "woe is me" story. During those times, it's hard for us to imagine how anything good could come from our suffering.

There was nothing pleasant about watching my grandmother waste away from Alzheimer's during my childhood and teenage years. I was so young when the disease took hold that most of my memories of her are of her forgetfulness. I know that she knew my name at some point because my mom told me so. but I don't actually recall her ever calling me by my name. I only have faint recollection of her being mobile without any type of aid. More pressing in my memories are her going from a cane to walker, and then to being completely bedridden in our dining room. I remember how exhausted my mother was as a widow trying to take care of her children and her rapidly declining mother. I remember trying so hard to alleviate her tiredness by doing all I could to take care of my grandmother, even when I was grossed out. I'd help clean out the bedsores that inevitably came no matter how many times we turned her or changed her or dressed her more tender spots. I also vividly recall feeding her one painstaking spoonful at a time— until she forgot how to swallow and then had to be fed intravenously. I couldn't understand how a loving God could possibly allow someone to suffer so much for so long. Ten years was a long time to spend on the process of dying. During that time, I developed an unhealthy fascination with death and the process of dying. I couldn't imagine a worse fate than to lose one's faculties. What good could possibly have come from all that suffering?

It wasn't until I was an adult and could look back on that time more holistically that I realized the strength of her faith that was on display. There's one memory of my grandmother that is more poignant than any of the others, and it happened on the day she died. This woman, who had forgotten how to eat, talk, or do anything, began to praise God in the clearest voice I'd ever heard. She sang her favorite spiritual songs, which had obviously been so embedded in her spirit that even though her mind was gone, they were still there. You see, although my grandmother couldn't remember her family, or how to do anything, she never forgot God. Her faith was what carried her through those ten years. I didn't understand it then. I thought she was alone, trapped in a decaying mind, but she wasn't alone. God faithfully walked with her every bit of those ten years, and for one day He allowed us to see His constant presence with her. Fast-forward twenty years to my recovery period from a ruptured brain aneurysm. How comforting to know that I wasn't alone as I battled with my own mind. On the days when I battled to find the right words to express what I was thinking or feeling, I knew that God knew. In those moments when I was so emotionally flooded that all I could do was cry, moan, or groan, God knew. I needed that understanding in that moment, just like I would need that understanding two years later when my mother succumbed to a brain aneurysm, and we had to make the heart-wrenching decision to terminate life support. How comforting to know that she wasn't alone in her comatose state. Today, as I think through all the times that I often have to stand alone for one reason or another, I know that I'm really not alone

My character was deeply influenced during those ten years my grandmother wasted away. Watching my mother faithfully care for my grandmother over all those years taught me about the sacrificial cost of true love. My mother had just turned forty when she became a widow with children to raise on her own, and then she had to care for her ailing mother. My mom had no knowledge of how long she would be in this situation. Yet she made the hard choice to pour out her love on us and on her mother at the same time as she reeled from the weight of losing the love of her life. She could've decided to focus on herself, to turn inward, or to give up. I'm sure she had days where giving up would've seemed easier. I know she had hard, lonely days. I saw the effect that her toil had on her health. Without a doubt, those days were a contributor to her need for a pacemaker in her fifty. But her love wouldn't allow her to opt out. She stayed, and she fought day after day, year after year, to make a life for us. She fought day after day, year after year, to take care of her ailing mother. She fought day after day, year after year, to hold onto her faith as she was left to journey through some pretty hard times without as much support from family members as she had hoped for. Somehow, in the midst of all this fighting, she managed to find enough love to open her home to others who were going through their own hard times. I couldn't begin to count how many people called 1913 Converse Street home over the years. Some came and stayed a few months, and some stayed a few years. It didn't matter how much food was on the table or in the cupboards—she didn't turn anyone away. You always knew that you had an open door with Sister Mary (as many adults who came into our home called her), Aunt Mary (as others called her), or Mom (as many others called her). My mom had a hand in raising many more children than she had given birth to in the natural. She could've gotten bitter about the hard hand life had dealt her, but she didn't. She chose to focus on the good that she could do with what she had available to her. She didn't have much money, but she did have an endless supply of love and hope, and she dished them out pretty liberally. She fought, she overcame, and she was rewarded, but those rewards came after many, many years of sacrifice. She eventually got to see her children, both natural and spiritual, go on to become military leaders, engineers, computer scientists, business leaders, entrepreneurs, and more. This loving sacrifice continues to speak to me even now as I sit here and type this up. My mother didn't leave a financial legacy; rather, her legacy was a life well lived through difficult times. Her greatness is not measured in financial wealth but in the depth of her character that then went on to influence many others.

Like my mother, my character has been forged through some pretty hard times, not of all which are mentioned in this book. I'd love to say that my life became easier when I accepted Christ as my Lord and Savior, but that was not the case. I came to faith on Father's Day 2000. My brother Anthony, whom I adored, died in his sleep on January 25, 2001. That was one of the worse calls of my life. In September 2001, not long before 9/11, I'd lose a child we'd hoped for and tried to have for a long time early in the second trimester of pregnancy. Just a few months later, we'd learn that my father-in-law had lung cancer. In July 2002, we'd bury him. A few months later, we'd learn that our goddaughter had leukemia; we'd bury her in January 2003. In between those times, one of my husband's closest friends would be murdered in a robbery attempt, and one of my son's football teammates suddenly died. To say that is was a long season in our life would be an understatement.

It was during this period of my life when my theme song became "Trading My Sorrows." A few versus, which are biblical in origin, spoke to me specifically.

> I've been pressed but not crushed, persecuted not abandoned. Struck down but not destroyed. I've been blessed beyond the curse because His promise will endure; and His joy is going to be my strength. Though my sorrows may last for a night, His joy comes in the morning.

I needed this reminder. I needed to know that my suffering was temporary; even if it lasted twenty years, it was still temporary in light of eternity. I didn't set out to become an overcomer with a testimony that might inspire others. I merely strove to be there for my family. I knew they were hurting every bit as much as I was. I knew my husband was in pain. I knew my kids were in pain. I knew that I couldn't afford to slip away because they needed someone to love them through the hurt, and I was that person. I knew I couldn't give up because I didn't want them to give up. So often our path to greatness is just that simple. I didn't keep going because I saw some great destiny up ahead. I kept going because I had to keep going. I got through one day, and then through the next day, and then through the next day. I got a little bit stronger, and then a little bit stronger, and then a little bit stronger.

Then the bottom of my world fell out. I will never forget the call that came on Thursday, December 11, 2008, just one week after my thirty-eighth birthday. My mother had a hemorrhagic stroke (brain bleed) and was comatose. My sister asked how quickly I could get to Pittsburgh. My mother's death was the beginning of a dark period for me that would last until October 2011. I would experience even more heartbreak as I went through experiences which I care not to recount within these pages, even as I was still coping with losing my mother. I would suffer through a deep, dark depression that almost cost my life. I wound engage in risky behavior the likes of which I would've never imagined were possible, and that could have cost me everything I had worked for my whole life. Every fiber in my being wanted to give up, but I didn't. I had pushed up against the very limits of my emotional, spiritual, and physical strength. I had nothing left. I was empty. If you've ever pushed yourself beyond your physical boundaries in pursuit of an athletic achievement, you know what it feels like to not believe you could take another step. You know what it's like to have every muscle and every bone in your body ache. You feel like you've exhausted every bit of reserve you've had. And then something happens. An inner resolve emerges that you didn't know was there. You know you can't give up, though you don't know how you'll go on. You simply know that you have to go on. So you take that next step; even if it's only gets you an inch closer, you're closer. You inch your way to the finish line if you have to, but you get there. And when you do, you look back in awe. You made it. You've pushed through, and now you're stronger. That's what I had to do during this dark period marked by a soul-gripping depression that sought to destroy me completely. I had to keep going one moment, one day at a time.

So often our path to greatness is just that simple. You don't keep going because you see some great destiny up ahead. You keep going because you have to keep going. You purpose to get through each moment, each hour, and each day. Days turn into months and as time passes you get stronger. The pains and hurts of the past do not go away but they are no longer able to paralyze you. And then you look back and see who you used to be and who you are now, and you're in awe at the progress. People look at your life and want to know your secret, and you search for some profound nugget you can share, but all you can come up with is that you just kept going by the grace of God. How do you climb a mountain? You climb it one step at a time. How do you persevere during hard times? You persevere one moment, one thought, one decision, and one day at time. Your focus isn't on greatness, but it is the result.

During this hard journey, you will regularly experience failure. Some failures will pass quickly; an unkind word may be forgiven just as quickly as it is spoken. Some failure will linger longer; a broken friendship may not be restored until years later. And some failures may stay with you for a lifetime. Each failure provides an opportunity to grow and take another step on your journey to greatness if you allow it. If you're willing to humble yourself enough to admit that you failed, you can begin to grow. One way to capture these growth moments is through journaling. The beauty of journaling, beyond giving you an opportunity to reflect on your feelings and experiences and put them in perspective, is that you can look back over them. You can see both your successes and your failures and how both contributed to your character-building journey. When you fail, you have a choice to make. You can obsess over that failure and allow it to consume you such that it derails you from your journey (more on that later), or you can choose to pick yourself back up, learn from that failure, and get back into the fray. Failure shouldn't be something you lose sleep over. Instead, it should be something that you embrace with the full expectation that your failures will serve a purpose both today and in the future. You should expect to grow into a better person because of your failures. You should expect your failures to better prepare you to help someone else in life. You should expect to be able to use your failure to speak hope to others.

I wish someone had told me when I was younger that failure was a healthy part of life and that I needed to learn how to embrace it. I wish I had known how much value failure could contribute to my character-forming process. Now, when people fail me (as they inevitably will because we're all flawed), instead of getting offended, I see it as an opportunity for both of us to grow and for our relationship to be strengthened. My hope is actually encouraged because there's an opportunity for a breakthrough. Now, that doesn't mean that I want to fail or that I want others to fail. I don't go around setting myself or others up for failure. I work quite hard trying to set myself and others up for success. I don't need to chase failure. If we're living the life destined for us, failure will come.

I like to consider myself a kind, compassionate, and sensitive person. Yet there are times when my actions have been anything but kind, compassionate, or sensitive. There is a memory that lingers with me to this day that reminds me of how easy it is to turn a blind eye to someone else's pain because it's inconvenient to me. I remember the day as if it was yesterday. I was returning to the office after having run a lunchtime errand. As I walked down the street, I noticed a young woman sitting on the sidewalk with a bewildered and desperate look on her face. Two young kids were with here, a boy and girl; I'm assuming they were her children. One was standing beside her while the other was also sitting on the sidewalk.

As my eyes locked upon the woman, I felt a draw to her as if I should walk up to her and talk to her, find out what was wrong, and point her to someplace where she could get help. But then I thought about my schedule. I had a meeting to get to, and I wanted to check e-mail and make a few phone calls before that meeting, so I walked by her. I looked back a time or two, each time thinking that I should go over to her, but I didn't. I allowed my schedule to interfere with an opportunity to pour love into someone who was obviously hurting. When I left the building to head to my meeting, she was gone. I don't know what happened to her. I will likely never know what became of her or whether she received the help that she needed. I hope that there was someone who came after me and who was moved into action by compassion. I failed that woman that day. I failed to do the good that I knew that I could do because I was too focused on myself and my agenda. My response to her was anything but compassionate or sensitive. That incident was a character-revealing incident for me. We need those on our journey. They reveal gaps between the person we believe ourselves to be and the person we actually are; only then can we begin to grow. Character revelation proceeds growth, so expect that on your journey.

I would love to say that after that failure, I never ignored the obvious need of a fellow person, but that's not true. There were still times after this incident that I failed in compassionate action when it was in my power to take such action. Often this failure was not because my compassion meter was too low; it was because I lacked any open time (margin) or was too weary to be of assistance to anyone. When

I saw people in their pain, I cared; I was simply too stretched to do anything about it. I was failing them once again but for a different reason. My heart had been dealt with, but now I had to deal with my schedule. After dealing with my margin issue, God took that persistent failure and turned it into something that could help others. My awakening to this controllable cause of my failure birthed my first book, *The Power of Rest*. The issue of margin and the process I went through to regain time for compassion is explored fully in that book. That failure became a character-forming process for me.

There were also times, even after that incident, when I allowed the extensiveness of the needs of humanity to overwhelm me into inaction. I failed not because my compassion meter was too low or I lacked margin, but because I had become so aware of all the suffering that I became fatalistic in my attitude. Tragedies are a dime a dozen in our society. This world is not lacking in war-torn nations with displaced refugees, human oppression, famines and food shortages, or homes destroyed by floods, fires, and other natural disasters. Human trafficking is on the rise, as is drug-addictions, drug-related crimes, and orphaned children living in squalor condition as a result of the addiction crisis. In the midst of so much inevitable suffering, why bother? Think about that. Despite that heart-wrenching experience with that woman, I could still look upon suffering and not spring into action. It wasn't that I didn't care; I simply believed that there was little I could do to make a difference. I was failing people not because I was hard-pressed for time. I was failing people because I didn't believe that I could help them. It was my own self-limiting thoughts of what helpfulness looked like that had become the issue. It was the same failure but a different cause that required a different response. I had to cut off that which was feeding all my negativity, which meant turning off the television, especially the news. Once I stopped watching the news and started spending time learning people's stories, I was reconnected with a hope that I hadn't realized I had lost. I didn't understand the power of hope until I listened to someone's story and responded simply by sharing my own. I didn't give people anything of tangible value. I didn't do anything that changed their circumstances, but their countenance changed. I realized then that when we have hope, we can endure just about anything. When we have hope, we can muster a strength that we never thought possible. When we have hope, we're able to speak life into people. We're able to give others hope because of the hope that we have and that's powerful. It was that realization that set my down the coaching path. It was failure once again, and what I learned on reflecting upon it, that was used to refine my character. I learned how to focus on the possible, even in the midst of difficult circumstances.

As you journey on your own path to greatness, you will encounter failure, and you will also encounter limitations. These are not the same thing. Failures are a result of decisions we make. Limitations arise because of current life circumstances or our perceptions of our own usefulness. On your journey, you will inevitably encounter a need you're not in position to meet. You may find yourself in a season of life where you don't have the financial resources or time to give as you would like. You may find yourself in a season of life where your burgeoning self-awareness and emerging appreciation of your talents and abilities create a desire to engage in societal issues, but your family commitments don't allow you to pursue open opportunities. You may find yourself feeling ill-equipped to offer assistance in any way. These are all limitations. They only become failures when you allow them to prevent you from doing what you are able to do in the moment. Regardless of where you're at in life, you have something of value to give to someone else. Your limitations do not set you up to fail. You do not need to stress over those limitations. You can be great right in the midst of them.

On your journey, you also don't need to fear whether you will fail. You will fail. Failure is inevitable because the path to greatness will, by necessity, push you outside of your comfort zone so that you can have the character revealing, character forming, and character refining experiences that you need to have to become who you are meant to be. You will be stretched beyond your breaking point. The path forward will not always be clear. You may take a misstep or two as you wade into new territory. Ultimately, you will have to learn to embrace trial and error and become resilient in the process. Your role in meeting the needs of your follow man will be uniquely suited to you. You're not meant to walk the exact same path as someone else because you're not someone else. This means that no one can actually lead you on your path; it's one that you'll have to discover on your own. Think of it as your own expedition journey made up of two parts, mapped and unmapped. The mapped parts of your journey are the paths that others have already traveled. You have the benefit of learning from them. They may have even paved a road to make it easier for those that follow. The unmapped parts are those parts of the journey that are for you to wade through with your sickle and cut down the weeds. Others can encourage you. They can coach you and support you. But you must do the hard work of forging down the path. You must sweat it out. Even with encouragement, you will likely feel fatigue and wonder whether you're on the right path. You may be tempted to quit. At those moments, your commitment to the character-forming process will show. If you understand that perseverance is success in and of itself, you will continue on. If you understand that sometimes you have to take action even if you don't feel like it, you will continue on. If you understand that great things are accomplished over a lifetime, you will continue on. If you prepare yourself for your journey even though you don't know where it will take you, you'll understand. And there is a way that you can prepare yourself for the journey. Despite the uniqueness of each person's journey, there is a consistent set of actions that everyone can take to better prepare themselves. These actions include broadening your awareness, scoping out the path, and establishing boundaries and safeguards.

BROADEN YOUR AWARENESS.

There are rhythms to life of which we need to be aware so that we are prepared to face them. How is it that seven children, who were born to a man and woman who did not possess a college education and who were raised in a working-class community that was experiencing the ravages of closing steel mills, could imagine themselves with college educations and professional careers? How is it that these same seven children could imagine themselves being successful in a world where racial tension still existed? In part, this phenomenon was able to occur because our worldview was not limited to our immediate circumstances or environment. We were exposed to a much broader world then what we could taste or feel in the present. This broader awareness not only sparked a passion in us for something greater but also grounded us in the reality that something greater was going to take a lot of work, persistence, and rugged determination. We were encouraged to dream. We were encouraged to learn our history (both American history and African history). We were encouraged to understand the way the world worked. We were encouraged to get an education and to take full advantage of the doors that it opened. We were encouraged to fully participate in the civic structure that is the backbone of our nations. Politics were discussed in our house. Current events were discussed in our house. Poverty was discussed in our house. We were expected to vote, and we were expected to use our voice for social justice. Our responsibility to our immediate family and to the greater church community was also discussed in our house. We were expected to grow up to be responsible adults who made positive contributions to society and stayed on the right side of the law. We were expected to be thankful for what we had and to cheerfully give to those who were less fortunate, even when we didn't have everything that we wanted. We had a roof over our heads, clothes on our backs, and food on our table. As long as that was true, we had blessings that we could share with others.

However, will all that said, we were also grounded in harshness of our world. The reality of being black in a recently desegregated America was not hidden from us. There was no sugarcoating in our household. We were told that we would we face trials and obstacles if we decided to live out our dreams simply because we were black. We were told that there were people who would work against us for our failure rather than our success. We would need to develop thick skin if we were going to stay the course. We were told that we would be discriminated against and unjustly accused, and we'd have little recourse. We were warned that there would be some people who wouldn't care how much we knew, how polite we were, or what abilities we had; they would only see one thing. We knew that we'd face harsher punishments for our failures than our white counterparts. That's the way the world was, and though we could rile against it, we couldn't afford to ignore it and act as if it was not. We were also told that there were people and situations that we should avoid if we're going to stay on the path to success. Some of these lessons came in the form of wise sayings, such as:

- Bad company corrupts good morals. We knew that our friends could influence our future. Whom we chose to spend our time with during our middle school and high school years mattered. What activities and habits they encouraged in us mattered.

- Be careful who you listen to; not everyone has your best interests at heart. We knew that all advice was not created equal; not everyone who smiled to our faces was our friends. We were taught to be skeptical and listen to our intuition.

- Stay alert and on your guard; your enemies are waiting for an opportunity to trip you up. There really was no such thing as letting your hair down or being off the clock. You were always on the clock because you were black living in white America.

- You can catch more bees with honey than with vinegar. In other words, kindness was always more effective than bitterness and scheming.

We learned that faith doesn't make life a cake walk. God is not a fairy godmother waiting to hand you everything you ever wanted in life. Your faith will get you through hard times, but it will not prevent them.

Some of the lessons came in the form of testimonials and stories. We heard the stories about people's lives that were derailed by drug abuse, but we also heard stories about people who went back to school to get their degrees after raising families. We heard the stories about black friends and family members who were beaten or even killed in racially motivated attacks, but we were also allowed to bring white friends into our home, and they were welcomed and accepted. We were not shielded from the reality of death. We knew that tomorrow was not promised, that death was final, and that funerals were designed to help the grieving obtain closure. But we also knew that life, no matter how short, was a gift to be cherished and enjoyed. It was also made very clear to us that although we may wish for and work toward change, we still must deal with the realities of today. Our reality was that we didn't have extra money, which meant we had to work if we wanted to get the things that we thought we deserved. I started my first paying job at twelve and have worked ever since. I worked while I was in college even though I was also a single mother at the time. My sister worked her way through college; she now has two master's degrees. One of my brothers spent twenty years in the navy before going to college to get his bachelor's degree in business. I and all of my siblings have made mistakes in our lives, but these lessons have stayed with us. We were able to bounce back from our mistakes, continue to chart our course, and stay on our journeys because we believed that there was something greater yet to be realized. We knew that we couldn't stop until we reached the full height of character that should be our aspiration. We may not have fully understood all the obstacles we would face, but we did understand that we had to persevere through them to achieve our goal. We weren't able to connect character development to a growing spiritual maturity, but we did understand that there was a development process that happened over time. We knew that failure wasn't permanent and that overnight success wasn't really overnight.

So what does this have to do with you? How do you apply this idea of broadening your awareness to the rhythms of life? Let's start by asking a simple question. When do you expect to die? That may seem like a morbid question, but it points to a reality of life that is true for every person: our time on this earth will come to an end. Have you dealt with that reality? Have you considered what you want the end of your story to be? If you haven't, what stops you from doing so? Death is not exactly dinner table conversation, but perhaps it should be placed on the menu on occasion—not in a morbid way but in a very practical way. We've been given the blessing of life for a short period of time. What are we going to do with it? We don't need to wait until we're at a loved one's funeral to grapple with the meaning of life or our express purpose. We can do it right now without a life-altering crisis.

Now let me ask you another question. When was the last time you put yourself in a position where failure was a real possibility? A life-sized dream will require taking risks to realize. You don't become a best-selling author by writing blog articles for a few friends to read. At some point in time, you have to write and publish a book. As soon as you do, you risk rejection and harsh criticism. You don't become a business leader by simply punching the clock each day. At some point, you have to stop out and lead. As soon as you do, you run the risk of making a bad decision, and you open yourself up to harsh criticism. You don't excel in loving others, being compassionate, and pouring out kindness in service to others without taking a risk that you will be hurt, taken advantage of, misunderstood, or ridiculed. Pursuing any type of goal worth pursuing requires taking risk. Regardless of whether you're ever in a titled position or ever have a public audience, you still have to take risk to become who you're meant to be. Trying to protect ourselves, our spouses, or our children from any possibility of failure or hurt feelings is not compatible with achieving a life of greatness. Although done with good intention, it stunts character development. The ability to bounce back from failure and overcome emotional hurts without becoming bitter is a part of journeying toward greatness. We call it resiliency, and a lack of it has obstructed many people's character formation.

I'm going to ask you one more question before we move on. When was the last time you saw people? I mean truly saw them—their brokenness, their hurts and pains, their shattered lives and shattered dreams. If you live in the suburbs like me, it's easy to keep yourself in a bubble. All you have to do is go to work, come home, park your car in the garage, go in through the side door, and stay in your house until morning. Then you can pretend that life is good, hard work is always rewarded, and bad things only happen to bad or lazy people. You have to get outside of your everyday world to truly see people and how difficult life can be and is for many. Now, if you happen to live in the urban city, that doesn't mean you're exempt from an inability to see people. It's easy to live in an urban setting and look past the homeless person on the corner or the single mother struggling next door to make rent and take care of her children. You may be in closer proximity to the issues, but that doesn't mean that you seem them. Seeing them requires that intentionality. You have to determine that you're going to broaden your perspective beyond the world in which you currently live. You have to determine that you will engage in conversations with people who are not like you, hang out in different places, wear different types of clothes, and think differently. As you do, the narrative that you've told yourself about life will change. Your dreams may change. You will find opportunities to take risks, and you have to decide whether to move forward or not. You have opportunities to display love, compassion, kindness, and service to others. In the midst of all of this, you will find a purpose that is greater than yourself. You will have fed the character formation process and be well on your way to greatness.

However, if you should shield yourself from the realities of life until you're thrust into the middle of a life crisis, then you may not have the skills to navigate that crisis and are far more likely to detour off track. If no detour is available, drugs or other pleasures may be used to escape the unpleasant reality. You may struggle to progress beyond your current position because the disillusionment or disappointment is too great to overcome. As a result, you spend ten years in a place where you were only meant to be for a short time. We do a disservice to society when we place ourselves or those we love in a bubble instead of broadening their perspective so they come to appreciate challenges, setbacks, and obstacles as a part of the development process. Encouraging ourselves and them to explore and experiment in a trial-and-error fashion, and learning from the inevitable failures that follows, positions us and them to stay on the intended path.

SCOPE OUT THE PATH.

Examine the path taken by others so that you understand how to grow your own toolkit. Although each person's journey is unique, it is not one that has to be traveled in ignorance. We are paradoxically complex yet simple beings. Our minds are incredible works of creation with underlying mechanisms that can be understood even if they can't be easily replicated. We're able to draw inferences from the experience of others that are relevant to our own context. We can learn how to succeed on our own paths by examining the path others have traveled. For example, we can learn what resiliency looks like by examining inventors like Thomas Edison, Alexander Bell, or the Wright Brothers. We can peer into the inner working of perseverance by examining the life of great missionaries such as Amy Carmichael, Hudson Taylor, or survivors of great injustices such as Immaculee Llibigazee, Malifa Oufkir, Ayaan Hirsi Ali, and Halimia Bashir. If we have the stomach for it, we can see what evil looks like up close by studying the atrocities committed by man against man during the Holocaust, the Rwandan Genocide, Stalin's Reign of Terror, the Killing Fields of Khmer Rouge (Pol Pot), and the reign of Mao Zedong. If we want to learn how to number our days, then we must be ardent students of both human nature and human history. The purpose of our studies is not to emulate another person; rather, our purpose is to understand the landmarks and landmines, the clear paths and the trip wires, and the quick access roads and the dead-ends. We can then use that understanding to inform our own journey.

Former drug addicts and victims rescued from human trafficking have bravely shared their stories for all to learn from. Why not value their courage by taking the time to listen to them and grow from them? Women who have suffered domestic abuse, teenage mothers, and so many others have made it a point to share who they have overcome. Why would we ignore these treasure troves of information on journeying through life?

I wouldn't have been able to navigate the business world without examining the journey of others. How would I have known how to conduct myself at a business lunch prior to committing a faux pas that could've been considered a career-limiting move? How would I have understood the concept of organizational politics before violating underwritten rules of behavior that could have placed me on a blacklist? How would I have understood the mechanics of business before making a costly financial or operational decision that could cost me my job? There is value in learning from personal experience. But if you can avoid car-damaging potholes, why wouldn't you?

We live in an age where we have access to tens of thousands of biographical accounts at our fingertips. You can read about leaders from bygone eras or leaders of today. You can listen to podcasts, watch videos, read articles, and complete online courses on any leadership principle that you want to study. We have the ability to engage mentors and coaches to provide us guidance as we need it. We don't have to wait several months for a letter to travel thousands of miles, we can interact real time through instant messaging and videoconferencing tools. There is absolutely no reason for us to travel our journey solo.

Despite all these resources, there will be experiences that are unique to us. There will be parts of our journey where we have to draw upon what we've deposited in ourselves to move forward. The key is that you've done the hard work of making deposits over time. You cannot withdraw from an empty account. You have to have built up some type of balance. The bigger the trial you face, the bigger the balance that you will need. In my life, I've found that it's the consistent practice of spiritual disciplines that establish the bank account balance I need to navigate my journey. I have a daily practice of prayer, reading, and meditation on biblical scripture. I observe a weekly Sabbath during which I journal and engage in deeper biblical study. I use quarterly weekend retreats and a longer annual retreat to reflect and refresh. Before I started these spiritual disciplines, I was erratic in my spiritual growth and withdrew far more than I deposited. I didn't spend time learning from others. I didn't recognize that those I most admired had a private spiritual discipline that sustained their public life. I didn't realize that I was missing this vital element in my character formation. That is why I was able to reach the point of desperation that I reached, which I share in more detail later in this book. Don't allow the same to happen to you. Reach out and learn from others. Involve them in your journey in whatever way is appropriate. Seek out wise counsel from trusted sources and heed the advice given. Don't rush into a decision where you have uncertainty, but also don't allow yourself to be paralyzed by indecision. Determine to take appropriate steps of faith and move forward with confidence knowing that recovery from failure is possible and will ultimately strengthen you.

ESTABLISH BOUNDARIES AND SAFEGUARDS.

Boundaries and safeguards are designed to keep us from crossing over into the danger zone. When you're driving on a mountain pass, and there's a guardrail separating you from a thousand-foot drop into a ravine, you don't test to see just how close you can get to the guardrail without falling over it. Instead, you try to keep a respectable distance between yourself and the guardrail. That's only prudent given the risk. In the same way, the boundaries and safeguards in our lives are designed to help us stay safely on the road.

Some dangers are more subtle and therefore more enticing than others. They may not even look like dangers, yet they can prevent us from doing the work we were meant to do and having the impact that we were meant to have. I enjoy coming up with fresh ideas. I could easily spend all my time imagining what could be without acting upon anything. But if I allowed myself to do that, then my influence would be minimal. I would be a dreamer with her head in the clouds, disconnected and disengaged from the realities of the world. Time management serves as a guardrail for me. I reserve certain time periods for ideation. The rest of the time is allocated to execution. In this way, I don't get out of balance, but I'm still creatively engaged and consistently innovating. The only way I can spend more time ideating, if I feel that's necessary, is to take a task off my to-do list. I don't allow myself to borrow the time and then deceive myself into believing that I will make it up later.

Similarly, I could live in the world of books. I have a goal to read fifty-two books a year. For me, this goal is about limitation not motivation. I could easily read more than fifty-two books a year, but I've noticed that when I exceed sixty books in a year, I begin to neglect other things that I need to do, like writing and spending time with family and friends. Setting a lower goal provides me some margin to reallocate reading time to an urgent work or relational demand. I could also concentrate all my reading into one genre instead of reading more broadly. Having at least one of my books each month come via recommendation or gift prevents me from becoming pigeonholed in my reading. It's one of the ways that I continue to broaden my awareness and expose myself to the different realities lived out by people around the world. I also have safeguards that are to protect me from the dangers of sexual temptations, drunkenness, and financial improprieties.

Boundaries and safeguards are highly personal in nature. They speak to your weaknesses, both shortcomings and overdone strengths. It will require discipline to establish these boundaries and safeguards, as well as a submissive heart to actually allow them to do their intended work. A boundary is useless if you're too stubborn to stop when you reach it.

Once you've broadened your awareness, scoped out the path, and established boundaries and safeguards, you're well on your way. You've begun to establish the right soil in which your character formation can occur. You've put yourself on the path of greatness. Life's all good, right? Not quite. As you forge down your unique path, you may also encounter detours. This is where life gets complex. Remember that we are living in a world of interconnected beings using free will to make decisions about their lives. At times, the decisions of others will come crashing up against your life, creating opportunities for you to get derailed from your path. At other times, people will intersect your path for what is only meant to be a short period of time. You will have to decide whether to part ways to continue on alone, which can be scary. And then there are times when opportunities are presented to you that seem right for you, but they may actually be detours intended to take you off course. Usually, these detours will be alluring with well-cut or semicut paths. When faced with these detours, you will have to decide whether to venture down that alternative path or whether to continue on the less attractive path that you're currently on. How do you make that decision? How do you know whether someone's path has come crashing into yours, whether it's time for you to veer apart, whether an opportunity is in your best interest, or whether the detour is a deterrent to reaching your destined greatness? How do you detect and prevent yourself from travelling down purpose-derailing detours (PDDs)?

CHAPTER 6

HOW DO I PREVENT PURPOSE-DERAILING DETOURS (PDDS)?

Some twists and turns in life are for your benefit (expedient), and some are to your detriment. Being able to distinguish the two will serve you well. Expedient detours (or turn-offs) are those that occur because they're the best course of action given the circumstances. An expedient detour happens whenever you're scanning the landscape and realize that there is an impediment that prevents you from taken the current path so you systematically look for an efficient route around the impediment. Generally, this happens when something crashes into your life that you weren't expecting. You haven't lost sight of your goal, and your planned course of action is designed to put you back on the designated path to your destination a soon as possible. In this sense, an expedient detour becomes an intentional part of your journey. You may not have anticipated it in advance, and in the beginning, you may even see it as an inconvenience and a source of frustration, or a source of incredible pain. In some cases, you may come to enjoy the detour as you experience sights that you wouldn't have seen otherwise. In those instances, though still inconvenienced, your attitude changes. You develop an appreciation for the detour. You can see the purpose in it. In other instances, the struggles associated with the detour are not put into focus until you get back onto the path. You realize that your detour prevented you from experiencing a trauma, protected your finances, or saved a relationship. When that realization occurs, you're inconvenience is brought into focus. Then there are those times where you never really come to fully understand the purpose of the detour. It seems pointless or unnecessarily painful. It's in those moments that you have to trust that it served a purpose.

In my own life, I've experienced all three types of expedient detours. The first would come early in my professional accounting career. I was a single mother, engaged to be married, and in the midst of closing on my first home when I resigned from my job for personal reasons. The resignation was prompted by a decision I had made a few months earlier to stay at the hospital and care for my four-year-old son, who was battling double pneumonia and confined within a plastic tent. His sickness happened to occur at our busiest time of the year and took me away from my job at a time when I was not allowed to miss. My absence was duly noted, and my lack of commitment to the job was reflected within my evaluations. My future within the company was questioned, and so I resigned. The timing of my resignation couldn't be worse, or so it seemed at the time. I guess you can say that sickness had decided to crash my journey, and suddenly I had to turn off the path that I was on. This resignation created a dilemma for me because I passed the CPA exam at the end of my senior year of college but still had about nine months of work experience required before I could get my CPA license. My qualification for my mortgage was based on both current income and expectation of financial stability because I was a soon to be a CPA with a job at a global accounting firm. How do you explain to the bank that all those factors they had used in their decision had changed? Fortunately, I didn't have to do much explaining. Before I had made it home the Friday I turned in my resignation, I had a contract job offer starting that Monday making about the same amount of money and guaranteed for at least a year, though I could end it at any time. By the end of the following week, I had a full-time job offer starting in two months, about the same time that my pay from my previous employer would end. Now I had two paychecks instead of one and plenty of money to cover the down payment on the house and initial moving expenses. During the two months I worked the contract job, I learned about the healthcare industry and third-party payment and reimbursement systems. That's knowledge that I still use today. Additionally, the experience I would get at the internal audit job I accepted would still qualify for my experience requirement because I would be supervised by a CPA. Not only would I stay on track to get my CPA, but I would also diversify my experience in accounting. And most important, I would have the flexibility I needed for my growing family. I was expecting another child and engaged to be married. It wasn't until much later that I realized that there were significant long-term benefits to the detour created when sickness crashed my party. This detour planted a seed of flexibility in me. I was learning how to remain centered in rapidly changing environments. It also planted a seed of faith in me. I wasn't yet in a relationship with God, but a seed of faith had been planted. I had exited the company at a good time in its history. Eight years later, my prospects would've been much worse because fraud would ultimately lead to the company's collapse. I had no idea what awaited me had I chosen to stay. In the end, my character grew simply because my son got deathly ill and needed me. It's not an experience I would've chosen, yet it played a pivotal role on my journey.

That seed of flexibility would be nourished as I learned to navigate the world of being a homeowner, a new mother, and a new wife all in the same year. It would flourish as the next detour hit my life. Once again it was on a Friday. That was when our entire department at PNC Bank would learn that the function had been outsourced, and as of that day we were no longer employed. Many of us would have an opportunity to interview with the outsourced provider, but there were no guaranteed positions. I still remember my response to this sudden news. I socialized all the rest of the afternoon—why not, right?

Then I went home and took out all my braids, relaxed my hair, and said, "Let's see what happens on Monday." I enjoyed the rest of the weekend with my kids and rolled with it. A sudden job loss crashed onto my path, and suddenly I had another turn-off on my journey. I had no idea how this would turn out or why this was happening after five years of faithful service. But it was, and all I could do was ride the wave, so ride it I did. I showed up at my interview Monday morning not sure what to expect. It couldn't have gone any better. I had the job offer before I left the building. The only problem was that I had sworn off public accounting after I left my first employer. I had no interest going back that direction after the experience, but here I was faced with the choice of entering back in or being without a job. The only difference was instead of being a single mother of one, I was now a married mother of three. I couldn't understand that direction; it didn't seem to make sense. I felt pressured to take the position because my income was a key part of our family's financial health. I wrestled with this decision for quite some time. I did not enjoy this rerouting in the road at all. After all the wrangling, I took the job. My logic was simple: take the offer and use the time to figure out what I really wanted to do. I reasoned that I could endure almost anything for a short period of time. I could take the job and then take my time interviewing for other positions. I didn't realize that this job offer would put me right back on my path to leadership in the accounting profession. Neither did I realize that this position would provide me the financial stability I desperately wanted. It wasn't until I was in the job for about a year that I began to see its potential. I've since traveled the world with Ernst and Young and built quite the resume. It's a resume that continues to serve me well in my current endeavors. Yet that's not its real benefit. My experience at that job did more than build a resume. It helped me grow my awareness of the world. It's where my empathy was developed. It's where I began to understand my responsibilities to others. It's what made me comfortable going on missions trips and engaging with other cultures. My character was developed in ways that I could've never anticipated. My appreciation for that experience continues to grow over time. This time, it was not a family member's illness but a strategic business decision that had created a turn in my journey.

Now, this next detour is a very interesting one. This detour would begin with a move to Columbus and participation in a leadership development program for potential partners, principals, and executive directors. I know that doesn't seem like much of a detour, but stay with me. It's a Thursday morning, and the area leaders have gathered to share their expectations of us and what we could expect as we went through the evaluation process. Out of nowhere, I would have the headache to beat all headaches. It was as if a bomb went off in my head. The whole room went mute, and my heart started to pound as if it was going to explode out of my chest. The ambulance couldn't get there fast enough. The ER doctor would make an observation that would save my life: I couldn't move my neck. A CT scan would show bleeding on the brain—an aneurysm had ruptured. I would take my first helicopter ride (aka life flight; not recommended) to a larger hospital where I could get emergency brain surgery (not sure there's any other kind) the following morning after being stabilized. Thus would begin my battle with mental and physical fatigue. Was I supposed to pursue promotion or not? Was it the right path for me, or was this a sign that I was on the wrong path? Was I supposed to slow down? Could the rupture have been triggered by the stress I was under with relocating? If I pursued promotion, could I actually perform? After all, I was finding it hard to concentrate, and I was absolutely exhausted doing my job at my currently level. Yet I had to make a decision quickly because applications were due. What was the right course of action? For the first time in quite some time, I was unsure of my destination. What I thought I wanted was right in front of me, but was it right? Was my aneurysm a sign to go a different path? What in the world could be expedient about an aneurysm and the long recovery process? Even today, some twelve years later, I battle mental fatigue and pressure-induced migraines. Perhaps the whole point of that "expedient" detour was that it slowed me down. Or the point was that it made me think about my purpose in life. Or perhaps it was that it set in motion the steps that would ultimately lead to entrepreneurship, vocational ministry, and resuming my creative passions. Or perhaps the point was that it created empathy in me for those with unseen physical disabilities. I really don't know for sure, and I sometimes wonder whether I couldn't have gotten to the same place without that detour. I certainly wouldn't wish that experience on anyone. It's not an experience I'd want to repeat. It was quite painful and continues to be so at times. There are days when my brain aches. I don't mean my head hurts—I mean my brain aches. It alternates between feeling like it's being crushed in a vice grip to feeling like someone is repeatedly jabbing it with an ice pick. I have had days where all I could do was curl into a ball and cry; the pain was so intense that painkillers were no help. There are times when I can't concentrate because it hurts too much. I also have episodes of auditory hypersensitivity and tinnitus, where whispers sound like screaming because they come through so loudly. At those times, silence is my best friend. My husband and children are no longer surprised when they come into the house and everything is off; they already know what type of day it's been. At times I get tired of experiencing all the pain, and I wonder whether this ongoing pain really serves a purpose. Unfortunately, I don't know the answer to that question, and I may never know the answer to that question. Yet I have to trust that there is a purpose served.

I didn't go looking for any of the detours that crashed my path; they found me. Yet it was expedient that they did because they helped me develop in a way that I wouldn't have otherwise, and they helped me to understand the greater purpose that there was for my life. That's the real beauty of expedient detour: they grow us. They're placed in our path, often unexpectedly and normally at inconvenient times because we wouldn't seek them out. You can't avoid expedient detours, and neither should you want to avoid them because they are a vital part of your character-development process. Though inconvenient and sometimes painful and frightful, these detours are to be embraced. We must resist the temptation to shortcut the development process.

Now, there are detours that we do want to avoid. These detours are what I've labeled as purpose-derailing detours (or PDDs). These are the detours that happen because of the bad decisions we make.

My mother had an admonition that used to irk me. She was always reminding us that we were free, but we were not free from the consequences of our choices, so we should choose wisely. Judging from how many times this phrase has been made into a meme or a Pinterest post, I'd say it's a pretty popular admonition. There are so many bad decisions that can detour us from our intended path. We can:

- Decide to use drugs or alcohol, setting ourselves up for addiction, criminal behavior, or sexual promiscuity.
- Decide to spend money recklessly, setting ourselves up for financial difficulties and making ourselves a more attractive target for predatory lenders.
- Decide to have sex outside of marriage, setting ourselves up for sexually transmitted diseases, unwanted pregnancies, and struggles with sexual sins that can carry into the marital relationships.
- Decide to engage in risky behaviors such as drinking and driving, texting and driving, and reckless behavior, setting ourselves up to inflict harm on others and/or face criminal violations that carry significant penalties, including imprisonment.
- Decide to dedicate ourselves to our jobs at the neglect and abandonment of family and friends, setting ourselves up for burnout, depression, and broken families.

I don't believe we set out to destroy our lives through bad decisions. Yet our families, our communities, and our societies are marred by the consequences of these bad decisions at an ever-increasing pace. PDDs abound. No one is immune from taking one or more of these detours. I have experienced burnout and depression. I've made bad decisions that could have cost me my family, my career, and my freedom. Why would I make those decisions knowing the potential consequences of them? Why would anyone?

We need to understand the psychology of PDDs if we're going to have any hope of avoiding them. Bad decisions are rooted in incorrect thinking and an unconstrained focus on self. We think that life is all about comfort, and so we pursue those things that make us feel good. We convince ourselves that no one is really hurt by our actions. If I want to have a drink, whose business is it but mine? And if I want to have two or three, whom am I hurting? We use acceptable words to describe our behavior—social drinking, enjoying adult beverages, taking the edge off, unwinding after a rough day, turning it up, or hanging out with the guys or gals. It all sounds so innocent and harmless. But the seeds have been planted.

Selfish wants are mistaken for needs, and so we spend an exorbitant amount of time, resources, and energy pursuing those needs. Over time, that pursuit begins to define us. Time with family and friends is sacrificed to obtain what we want. Rationalization sets in, allowing us to justify behavior that would've been unthinkable before. Healthy restraints are thrown off because they hinder us from doing those things that we believe will bring us pleasure. The marital covenant is no longer sacred. If someone else will bring you more happy pleasure, you reckon that you owe yourself that much. Life is too short, and you work too hard to not pursue him or her. Your heart begins to harden against any advice. Guidance, whether solicited or unsolicited, is labeled as criticism, judgment, and legalism. No one has the right to tell you what to do or not do. You are the master of your ship. The time it takes to travel this path, and the particular sins that wait to entrap you, varies. Instead of sexual sins, it may be drugs and alcohol, or gambling, or the many other vices that plague our society. However, the pathology is the same. Understanding that pathology is what enables us to avoid making the bad decisions that lead us down a path we will later regret. That's what we will now turn our attention to in hopes of arming us to lead a life of character.

ANATOMY OF THE WRONG PATH

Our journey down the wrong path begins rather innocuously. We're told that free thinking demands that we throw away any possible consideration of the existence of a grand design. Once we do that, we're left with believing that there is no defined purpose for man outside of what man defines for ourselves. If we're not part of a bigger story, then our efforts should be spent making as good a life for ourselves on this Earth as possible. Everything else builds upon our thinking about the source and meaning of life. Now, this is not a theology book or an apologetic discourse, so I will not recount the biblical account of the origins of the universe, of man, and of man's purpose. Instead, I will challenge you to ponder the following.

- Why are we surprised by the divorce rate when marriage has been reduced to two selfish people marrying with the expectation that the other person will meet all needs at all times? Either one person is going to be swallowed up into the other, or there will be continual conflict as dreams and wants collide. When there is no other expressed purpose for marriage but to make oneself happy by living life with someone whom you believe will bring you pleasure, what carries you through those times when that doesn't happen? What's your reason for staying when life together gets tough? But what if the process of two selfish people coming together to live life is designed to build character? Think about what that would mean when conflict occurs. You don't run away from the conflict; instead, you lean into conflict, learn how to communicate with one another, and navigate through it. Instead of acting on emotions, you learn how to love regardless of how you feel. Instead of demanding your way, you learn how to serve. The very traits that we so admire in leaders are often first developed within the marital relationship. Yet our self-focus demotes the marital relationship to nothing more than a decision we made that was in our best interest at a point in time—and that can be unwound once that best interest is no longer served.

- Why are we surprised by the increasing rate of addiction when elimination of boredom, discomfort, pain, and suffering has been elevated as a virtue? What options do you have when you don't get the promotion or lose your job other than to go have a drink or two? How do you process disappointments or trauma without heavy doses of medication? What purpose could possibly be served by suffering when the whole purpose of life is joy? But what if suffering serves to develop our character? What if the very act of weathering through the difficult times develops strength, fortitude, and patience? What if the traits we admire in leaders such as Abraham Lincoln, Mother Teresa, William Wilberforce, and Nelson Mandela developed in them because of the tragedies and setbacks they suffered in their lives? Without a grand design, such thinking makes no sense. Without a greater purpose, we have no reason to suffer through tragedies. It makes sense for us to detour onto a path that brings us comfort and joy, even if it's fleeting and requires a continual fix to maintain.

- Why are we surprised by abortion, declining birth rates, and absentee parents when parenthood has been reduced to satisfaction of the selfish desire to create an image bearer who can make you proud? In a world without a grand design, childbearing is something you do when it's convenient. But what if childrearing, much like marriage, was designed as a character-development tool? When that baby cries at 2:00 a.m., you learn the inconvenience of serving someone who doesn't operate on your schedule and can never pay you back. When you reprioritize your budget to buy things for your child instead of indulging yourself, you're learning how to put someone else's needs first. Servant leadership is the essence of parenting. It's ironic that so many leadership books have been written on servant leadership even as parenting has fallen out of favor in a self-indulged society.

A world where man is in ultimate control may seem like an ideal world, but it's really just the opposite. A man-controlled world where people are defining life for themselves and doing as they see fit is a world with many attractive but destructive detours. In this type of world, it's only logical to want to accumulate wealth so that you can lead a life of comfort and indulgence. For those attracted to accomplishment, it's only logical to accumulate as many awards, degrees, and wins as possible so that your circle of influence continues to grow and your name is elevated within that circle. Avoiding these attractive but destructive detours begins by acknowledging that there is a grand design initiated by a creative God who intentionally designed man and has given man an expressed purpose for being. As you understand the intended design, live within its boundaries, and submit to your expressed purpose, you journey along the right path. Your failures become growth opportunities. The struggles you encounter forge a depth of character often envied and sought after. Over time, you begin to appreciate the challenges of life though you may never actually seek out difficult times. If that sounds too good to be true, take heart; I used to think the same thing. I used to look at people like me who embrace failure and difficulties as if they had a horn growing out of the center of their head, a silvery white mane flowing down their back, and multicolored bow hovering above them—that is, a rainbow unicorn). I thought they needed to get with reality or get a grip. Clearly, they hadn't endured the trauma I'd endured. Well, here I am now, counted among them same people whom I would have scoffed at before. Here, I am saying that we can have joy in the midst of difficult life circumstances. We can love people who are difficult to love (some might even call them unlovable), even when we are hurting. We can honor our marital covenants even when the feelings aren't there. We shouldn't expect kudos and accolades for pouring ourselves out in service to others—we should just do it. We should expect to fail and expect others to fail, and we should encourage them when they do. Life isn't always going to go how we expect it to go or want it to go, and that doesn't have to send us into a tailspin. We can overcome those disappointments and setbacks. We don't need to fear inadequacy because we're fully capable of achieving our intended greatness. Yes, I am saying all those things. The errors in my thinking have been corrected. The mess I had made of my life has been cleaned up. The purpose that I have has been clarified, and I'm fully back on track on my journey. So I know beyond the shadow of a doubt that failure is not permanent. A messy life is not a death sentence. Something new can begin today if you really desire it.

If, by chance, reading this book is causing you to reflect on the mess you've made out of you, don't worry; we'll address it how to get back on track. If you've had character development moments and blew it, all is not lost. If you made those purpose-derailing detours I've mentioned, it's not too late to get back on track. If you haven't established boundaries, have pursued pleasure, and have thrown your marriage away, there is still a path for you.

What do you do now that you're offtrack? How do you get back on track? And then, how do you protect yourself from further destructive detours? That's what we turn attention to next.

CHAPTER 7

WHAT IF I'VE DETOURED OFFTRACK?

The reality of life is that the vast majority of us will take at least one unplanned, purpose-derailing detour that pulls us away from our path to greatness. Fortunately, these detours will only prevent you from reaching your destination if you stubbornly refuse to acknowledge you're offtrack and resist taking the necessary actions to get back on track. The longer you resist acknowledging your failure, the longer it will take back on track. However, getting back on track is possible. As we look at what it takes to get back on track, we're going to look at four different groups of people: those about to detour offtrack, those who have already detoured offtrack and are continuing on the wrong path, those who are in the process of being rerouted back on track, and those who have gotten back on track and want to make sure they stay there. A few personal stories are shared to show the transformation that is truly possible. There's nothing special about the individuals whose stories are shared other than that they were willing to allow the transformation process to work in their lives. These are stories that are not often shared. Unfortunately, this silence leaves people feeling as if they are too much of a mess and can't possibly achieve greatness. People who are about to detour offtrack have a lot in common with those who have already veered offtrack and can learn a lot from them.

Perhaps, in the learning, they can avoid the detour and stay on their intended path. But how do you know? How do you know if you're on the brink of detouring or if you're already detoured? Let's take a look at each group.

GROUP 1: ABOUT TO DETOUR OFFTRACK

Detouring offtrack often starts subtly with minor compromises and rationalizations. I don't know anyone who wakes up with the intention of becoming a no-name failure. I don't know people who hope that their lives will never matter and that they will never accomplish anything that makes a difference in anyone else's life. Perhaps you know those type of people, but I don't. Yet I do know plenty of people who are not living up to their potential. I have friends and associates whose lives are so wrapped up in acquiring the right title, status, and material possessions that they are completely immune to the world around them. I've seen people who confess to loving their families with all their hearts engage in adulterous affairs, abuse their spouses and children, and otherwise inflict harm and suffering on their closest friends and families. How did these people veer so far offtrack?

Robert Steinberg, a professor at Oklahoma State University, speaks and writes about a concept that he titles ethical drift. Though this concept really focuses on how good people can do bad things, we're going to look at drift from the perspective of someone who finds his life veering off course despite good intentions. At a relatively young age, one of my childhood friends introduced me to the concept of the five-finger discount. Intuitively, I knew that this five-finger discount was wrong—that it was really just stealing given a catchy name. I didn't join in with her on that day, but a seed was planted. One day I was in a store and really, really wanted a little trinket that I couldn't afford. (Remember: widowed mom raising her family, no extra money for frivolous things us kids "needed.") I just had to have it. I thought about that trinket. I thought about how good it would feel to have it in my possession. I thought about how much I would enjoy it and what I would do with it. And so I decided to help myself to it and justified it in my childish mind by saying that it wasn't my fault my father had died, and my mom had to work so hard to support us now that she was a widow. And I got away with it. A part of me wishes that I hadn't because my success made it easier to do it the second time and then the third time. Eventually, I did get caught and my mom was not happy. I was made to work off the cost of all that I had stolen, including all that had previously been undiscovered. And I'm glad that I was because my attitude about the five-finger discount changed. I had veered offtrack, but the proper amount of correction applied at a pivotal time prevented me from careening out of control. My mother's direct confrontation of my sin initiated a character-development moment in my life. She didn't let me get away with thinking that I was good when I really wasn't. She forced me to face the reality that I was doing something wrong. As a child, I didn't yet grasp the concept of rationalization or realize that there was a deeper issue at work in me (and indeed at work in all of us). I didn't understand that I couldn't just moderate my behavior but had to go to the root and pluck it out.

As I look back on my "self-discounting" days, I can clearly see that drift was at work. Although I knew that in most cases stealing was wrong, I was still able to justify my case as being different. I was able to find justification within the difficult circumstances that surrounded my life. My father had died tragically when I was eight years old. My mom struggled to finish raising us on her own. Money was tight. There was no provision for the extras that many of my schoolmates seemed to take for granted. No need to bother my mom—she was already weighed down by the burdens of care for us. And it wouldn't be missed anyway. It was just little stuff that probably didn't mean much to others but meant everything to me. And so on. Rationalization is easy once you get the ball rolling. It's like a snowball that picks up speed and size as it rolls downhill—until it triggers an avalanche that covers over or destroys everything in its path. Rationalization doesn't just happen with things we know we shouldn't do or with vices. Rationalization also allows us to veer offtrack with "good" things as well; we call this good intentions gone astray. It starts subtly and happens below our own level of awareness. If we're not in continual fellowship with other like-minded individuals who can point out our blind spots, we're likely to miss it. The character formation that leads to greatness happens in relationship. We cannot develop our character in isolation. We must have authentic relationships with people where we are presenting our true selves—no facades. We must allow ourselves to be known. We also have to be humble enough to allow other people to call us out when they see us even considering a path of compromise. We must give people permission to speak into our lives, and we need to have a variety of people in our lives, different generations, and different life circumstances. To believe that any one person alone is able to withstand the tide of popular culture that says life is all about how much pleasure you can accumulate now is like believing that you can stand on the shore as a tsunami approaches and not be washed away. Don't set yourself up for detour by isolating yourself and going it alone. Allow people to speak into your life. Submit yourself to one of the primary tools God uses to develop our character and relationships.

GOOD INTENTIONS GONE ASTRAY

In many respects, the drifting that occurs in our lives works the exact same way whether we are talking about vices or good things. We start out with good intentions. Perhaps we want to make enough money to be able to support our families and give generously to meet the needs of others. I think we'd all consider working to provide for ourselves and our families as honorable and noble. In fact, we're advised by Timothy 5:8 that anyone who does not provide for his own, and especially for those of his household, has denied the faith and is worse than an unbeliever.

However, somewhere along the way, if we're not careful and properly grounded, our noble purpose can become distorted, and our focus can shift from supporting our families to supporting our pleasures and desires. As we make more money, we may find ourselves giving less to charity because our "needs" have grown exponentially. We also have less time to volunteer because our work and our recreation take up more and more of our time. We have begun to detour, and without intervention, we will find ourselves leading a materialistic, consumeristic lifestyle that is all about me and mine. We will begin to believe that we are responsible for our own success, and if people worked as hard as we did, they could get the same result. When this shift in thinking happens, our hearts begin to harden against the needs of the community. We're able to look upon the homeless and not feel compassion. We see bums who need to ditch the drugs and alcohol, clean themselves up, and get jobs. They need to put in an honest day's work like everyone else and stop expecting society to take care of them. We're able to look upon prostitutes and actually believe that they prefer that lifestyle. If they really wanted to, they could walk away and start fresh. After all, there are welfare and vocational education programs with their name written on it and that our hard-earned money has already paid for in the form of taxes. We're able to snub our noses at ex-offenders fresh out of prison who are struggling to find jobs, and we believe that they just need to try harder. They simply need to fill out a few more job applications, or perhaps enroll in community college and get a meaningful education so that they're prepared to be productive members of society. We convince ourselves that we are justified in our indulgences. We've earned it with all those extra hours worked at the sacrifice of time with our families or enjoying our hobbies. Charity becomes either a luxury we cannot afford or a way to make us feel good about our indulgences.

When charity becomes a luxury we cannot afford, we begin to question the prudency of giving to charity at all, given our own "needs," We become really good at masking our selfishness under a cloak of prudence. Those additional vacations homes that we own are investments that will secure our financial future. All the artwork, antiques, and vacations are exposing our children and our children's children to different cultures. The different businesses that we invest in at ever-increasing rates are building wealth and leaving a legacy for our families. Empire building becomes the name of the game, and the bottom line trumps all.

So of course we become more demanding of the nonprofits which we give money to, but only so that we can assure that there's a sufficient return on investment and they're not wasting any of that hard-earned cash. We don't see the irony of wanting a detailed account of every penny given to charity while wasting hundreds of dollars each week on our own entertainment. We don't see the hypocrisy in splurging on our indulgences while asking the nonprofit to squeeze and stretch as much as possible. We don't feel the least twinge of guilt or conviction in giving expired food or clothes with rips or stains to charity because they should be happy with whatever they get. We ask the difficult questions to hold them accountable to a standard the likes of which we'd never want to hold ourselves accountable to, and we are never called out for it. We strain out a gnat while swallowing a camel (Matthew 23:34). When we've reached this point in our journey, we are fully offtrack and destined for a life of indulgence instead of a life of greatness. But where did it all start? Is there something you could've done to recognize this purpose-derailing detour before it was too late? What early warning signal could've alerted you to this unfortunate end?

Generally, this detour starts with rationalizing what we "deserve." As soon as we talk about what we deserve, we have a problem— we're looking inward instead of outward. We're focused on ourselves. We're already put ourselves at the center of the equation. Life has become all about us and what we are entitled to because we want it. We want respect, obedience, and trust, whether earned or not. We want a certain level of income, whether or not the employer can afford it. We expect to make enough to live in nice dwellings within nice neighborhoods, drive nice cars, and take nice vacations because we have college degrees. We look at these as separate issues, but they are not. What people seem to not see is that the root is all the same (and needs plucked out): we've engaged in rationalizations, and our good intentions have gone astray. The solution is also the same: a realization that our needs are few, that there's little that we deserve but much that we are blessed with, and that we should feel gratitude. It should also make us want to use those blessings in ways that benefit others. A heart of gratitude begins to pulls us from a self-focused view of life to an other-focused view of life. We begin to gladly look for ways to meet the needs of our brothers and sisters with no expectation of gain, recognition, or other ulterior motive. When we've begun to operate with that outward mind-set we're getting back on track.

If we're not able to come to this realization on our own, a situation may have to come crashing into our lives to get us to see how we have strayed. These wake-up calls come in all kinds of shapes and sizes, including job loss, illness, and marital troubles. We can choose to run from these wake-up calls, or we can lean into them, trusting the process of character formation that we are being subjected to for our own good.

ADDICTED TO DOING GOOD

We're just as prone to go off track when it comes to doing good. We may have a desire to address the suffering of people. Perhaps we're motivated by compassion to act. This compassion, just like working to provide for ourselves and our families, is noble and honorable and is an integral part of the gospel. In Isaiah 58:7–8, we see that God desires that we loosen the bonds of wickedness, break the yoke of oppression, divide our bread with the hungry, and bring the homeless poor to the house. James 1:27 advises us that pure and undefiled religion in the sight of God is to look after widows and orphans in their distress. We're further advised in James that faith without works is dead. Our faith will move us to compassionate action when we see a brother or sister in need. We will go beyond wishing each other well and do the good that we know to do and are able to do.

We begin to veer offtrack, however, when we become enamored with the feeling of doing good. We enter the danger zone when we fall in love with the thought of doing good and being seen doing good. We stop connecting with the humanity of the people we're serving; instead, they become statistics to quote and stories to trumpet to all who will hear. We become so infatuated with the publicity and goodwill generated by acts of kindness that we begin to discriminate in our good deeds. We begin to help those who are in the best position to bring us positive press while ignoring others. We go out to the places where we're most likely to be noticed while shying away from those places that are less noteworthy. We seek out ways to serve in very public ways while shunning service that is more behind the scenes. We can even rationalize this discrimination in the name of sound stewardship of resources: we can't help everyone, and we need to generate funds to stay on mission. So of course we're going to go to those places that will give us the greatest return. We begin to court people to be involved in causes based on the resources that they can bring to bear on the issue. We begin to change the language that we use so as not to offend anyone who may want to donate to the cause. We begin to change our value statements so as not to offend anyone who may want to volunteer for the cause. We begin to name-drop so that we can have the right doors open to us—all for the good of the organization, of course. After all, we have a mission to accomplish, and no funds equals no mission. We don't see the favoritism that we show because we mask it in business language. We're building a strong financial network. We're securing the financial future of the organization. We're establishing the foundation for growth. But what we've really done is veer offtrack, and if we fail to realize this, we may wake up one day to find that not only have we compromised our values, but we have also caused the organization to compromise its value to the point of being unrecognizable from where it started.

But where did it all start? Is there something you could've done to recognize this purpose-derailing detour before it was too late? What early warning signal could've alerted you to this unfortunate end?

Just like in the previous example, this rationalization begins with looking inward. The wording is a little different, though. Instead of saying "I deserve," we say words like *need, must,* or *else.* Be careful of statements like "They need me" or "I must do this or else." These are words that have turned the attention back to us in our desire for significance. It's a very subtle way of making us feel indispensable. It's self-exaltation, self-righteousness, and pride, and it's dangerous. It's a character flaw to which we are all vulnerable. Should we continue down this path, ignoring all attempts at correction, situations may crash our journey to help us get back on track. These wake-up calls come in all kinds of shapes and sizes, including job loss, illness, financial strain, and sudden changes in the business environment that render the services of the organization obsolete or of much less significance. We can choose to run from these wake-up calls, or we can lean into them, trusting the process of character formation that we are being subjected to for our own good.

THE BITTER PILL OF DISAPPOINTMENTS

Langston Hughes asked, "What happens to a dream deferred, does it dry up like a raisin in the sun or fester like a sore?" The Bible advises us that hope deferred makes the heart sick (Proverbs 13:12). Life is full of disappointments. Whether it's not getting the job or promotion you desired and seemed to deserve, being betrayed by a friend, or getting sick while on a much-anticipated vacation, life does not go as planned. But when the disappointments are bitter, they can take root in your soul and change your outlook on life. Perhaps a loved one dies young. Maybe you've found out you were barren after many years of trying to bear children. Perhaps your spouse deserts you for another person after decades of marriage. Maybe you received a negative medical diagnosis when you we're just going in for an annual check-up. Bitter pills are hard to swallow; they affect us at our core, often calling into question our very identity and purpose.

The dreams and goals that used to keep us fueled lose their power to engage. Hope and joy become distant memories. Pain becomes the constant companion. Criticism, sarcasm, and pessimism wrap around us like a shroud. Friendships wither under the strain. If you're lucky, you become a faint shadow of who you were meant to be. If you're not lucky, you become a different person whom you barely recognize. But where did it all start? Is there something you could've done to recognize this purpose-derailing detour before it was too late? What early warning signal could've alerted you to this unfortunate end? It would seem like this root cause is different than the other two examples, but it is not. Bitter disappointments pull us offtrack when we turn our focus inward. We go far beyond grieving, which is healthy, to wallowing in our sorrows, which is not. We wear the tragic circumstances of our life like a lapel pin. Everyone hears about it all the time. Pride, or excessive focus on self, is still at the heart of our response. Pride is such a devious little thing, masking itself in so many different forms. The formula is not what it would seem. This type of self-focus is circumvented through cultivating a grateful and thankful heart. When I was going through some of my most difficult moments, a gratitude journal kept me centered. Initially I didn't think I could find much to be grateful for; after all, I was in pain. But I was wrong. Take a look at this gratitude journal and see what resonates with you. Some of these entries are from 2014, and some are from 2015.

1. I'm thankful that God sees our potential and patiently leads us forward toward it. His mercies are new every morning and never cease to amaze me.

2. I'm thankful that it's never too late to change. Your tomorrow doesn't have to mirror your today, and relationships can be repaired.

3. I'm thankful for my mother-in-law and spiritual mother and all the love that she has poured into my live for the past twenty-two years from the time my husband and I first started dating. I couldn't ask for a better mother-in-law.

4. I'm thankful for God providing me a life partner who has walked with me and who encourages me through all of life's ups and downs, twists and turns.

5. I'm thankful for God giving me the privilege of parenting three amazing kids.

6. I'm thankful that I have a sister who has been there for me through thick and thin.

7. I'm thankful for the nieces and nephews that I'm blessed with on both sides of the family. I counted yesterday and the number now sits at sixty-six with at least one more on the way early 2015. And yes, I do know all their names, though I don't remember all their birthdays. And no, I'm not going to list them all on here.

8. I'm thankful for times of prayers where I have the privilege of entering into the throne room of God.

9. I'm thankful for people who are willing to dare the impossible and make it a reality so that our daily lives are made better.

10. I'm thankful for nature. There's little that compares to a beautiful sunrise or sunset, or a gentle breeze coming from the ocean shore.

11. I'm thankful for intelligence. The gift of reading, learning, and exploring our world is a gift to be cherished always.

12. I'm thankful for health. Though I have my issues, I'm healthy enough to enjoy life on this beautiful planet.

13. I'm thankful for hope. It's been a very long summer, and the storm isn't over yet, but I have a hope that's not dependent on my circumstances.

14. I'm thankful for books. Reading is more than fundamental. Reading books helps us to relate to events and people across time, geographical distances, and cultures. Reading broadly but selectively opens our minds.

15. I'm thankful for work. We were meant to be productive. As my momma always cautioned us, "An idle mind is the devil's playground."

16. I'm thankful for people who are willing to speak truth into my life even when I don't want to hear it. These are true friends.

17. I'm thankful for music. Music speaks to my soul and shines a light into my innermost being. Music helps me to reveal myself to others. Music is truly the universal language.

18. I'm thankful for visual works of art and the artists who create them. Painting, sculpting, and other visual expressions reflect the creative masterpiece that we simply call life.

19. I'm thankful for our five senses. The ability to see, to hear, to touch, to taste, and to smell provides so many rich experiences. When I have a bad cold, food just isn't the same because I can't smell it.

20. I'm thankful for our range of emotions. When I had my first son, I didn't think I could love any more than I already did. Then my family grew, and so did my love. I can laugh in the midst of pain and cry tears of joy or of sorrow. Life is all the more interesting because of it.

21. I'm thankful for nights like tonight: quiet, free summer evening where I can just be. No commitments, no rush to meet a deadline, no plans.

22. I'm thankful for our amazing brains. We do so many things without ever having to think about them. Could you imagine having to remember not only to breathe, but all the steps involved in such an action? Or having to remember to produce hormones and produce them in the right quantities?

23. I'm thankful for mobility. I went for a four-mile jog/walk today and threw in a bit of weightlifting and stretching just because I was restless and my energy was waning. Moving about cleared my mind and got my energy flowing.

24. I'm thankful for modern conveniences. My day was so much easier because I could load my laundry into the washer, load the dishes into the dishwasher, and let them do their thing. We have self-cleaning ovens, deep-cleaning carpet cleaners, and so much more.

25. I'm thankful for honest, caring people who will go out of their way to do the right thing. A little bit ago, I lost a check that I had written out with everything except the "pay to" field completed. Imagine my surprise and delight when I received that check in the mail with a handwritten note from the person who'd found the check. The check was fully negotiable and she chose to return it.

26. I'm thankful for the leadership of Pastor Dave Gross and Pastor Kay Gross. Their humble, servant nature; impeccable character; and drive and energy continue to challenge and encourage me.

27. I'm thankful for a group of ladies who are willing to cover me in prayer. I appreciate it more than words could ever say.

28. I'm thankful for a mother who modeled love of God, love of family, and love of people. Her unconditional and sacrificial love continues to inspire me.

29. I'm thankful for the scientific discovery process. We live in an amazing world whose mysteries we have barely even begun to discover. Scientific inquiry is a God-given gift that allows us to unlock the marvels of creation and increases our awe and reverence for the creator.

30. I'm thankful for the digital technologies that allow us to communicate with individuals around the world. We are a social people in need of deep social connections. I'm willing to try out any technology that improves our abilities to develop and nurture meaningful, healthy relationships with people of difficult cultures.

31. I'm thankful that our church has times of celebration, like today's Labor Day picnic, that allow us to come together as a church family celebrating the goodness of God and the joy of community.

32. I'm thankful that God has gifted Monique with the talent for and love of baking, and I get to watch it. Watching her bake is like watching art in the making. She's so intensely focused and precise as to the outcome that she wants. Her commitment to excellence shines through as bright as a full moon on a dark, starless night.

33. I'm thankful that God has given Monique a love of children. I enjoy watching her come to life as she talks about the children in her daycare and the children at church. She's fully in her element when she's pouring into children. She knows how to talk to them. She knows how to develop them. She knows how to lead them. I'm in awe as to all that God is doing through her.

34. I'm thankful for the time that I had with Amy today. Thank you for connecting us and for speaking into her life. I thank you for all that you are working in her as she seeks you and your plan for her life. I thank you for her faithful obedience in the midst of difficult circumstances.

35. I'm thankful for the way you're ministering to those who have come to Radiant Life to make it their home after their church had to close. Losing your church home is not easy. Thank you for allowing us to come alongside them and welcome them as our brothers and sisters.

36. I'm thankful for decaf coffee and cappuccino. It's such a refreshing drink to start off my morning. I enjoy the flavor and its symbolism. For me, this drink reminds me that God is sovereign, and I can afford to take the time to enjoy a cup of coffee.

37. I'm thankful for the warmth of the sun and calm, clear, blue skies. The wispiness of clouds is always a marvel. They seem so soft and gentle, yet great storms emerge from their midst. They seem like you should be able to just pass right through them, yet their resistance is the bane of many airplane travelers.

38. I'm thankful for my typing classes. When I took them in high school, I had no idea that I would use my typing skills on a daily basis. I didn't understand that computers would become so integral to our lives and keyboarding would become a critical life skill.

39. I'm thankful for the maturity that I'm seeing in Dana Jr. He takes responsibility for his actions. He's become dependable and responsible.

40. I'm thankful for Dana's decision to take some vacation time. He weighed the options available to him and made a wise choice to take time away instead of quitting his job.

41. I'm thankful for my husband placing his hand on my head and saying a prayer over me. I don't know what prompted it, but the thought warms my heart.

42. I'm thankful for my husband's support in ministry. He doesn't get upset about my time outside of the home.

43. I'm thankful for the provision that God has made to allow us to keep this home. I'm relieved that I don't have to pull my husband or children away from what has become their family home.

44. I'm thankful for opportunities like this, where I can glance over at my husband's sleeping body. He's so at peace.

45. I'm thankful for bacon; the taste of it is so succulent. My tongue comes alive in anticipation.

46. I'm thankful for The Truth Project. Completing this study has further anchored my faith and better equipped me to defend my faith with others. I continue to be amazed by this study week after week. I would add this to my thankfulness list every week if I wasn't trying to not repeat items.

47. I'm thankful for the opportunity to serve as a small group leader. I never realized what a privilege it would be to lead a group of women in the study and worship of God.

48. I'm thankful for cooler weather. This summer without air-conditioning was challenging. Especially the past week were temperatures soared into the nineties.

49. I'm thankful for a team that's willing to press in there and get done what needs to get done.

50. I'm thankful for my corporate credit card. I can't imagine doing my current job without a corporate card and having to advance all the expenses from our personal funds or personal credit card.

51. I'm thankful for having the funds required to purchase a decent used car to replace my husband's vehicle, which we totaled. It's a different make and model, but only one year older than what he had, with almost 40,000 fewer miles and no exhaust issues or other immediate repairs required—and no car payments.

52. I'm thankful for how my team, both new and old, has stepped right in and hit the ground running. Thanks for sending them to me.

53. I'm thankful for the opportunity to shape the accounting profession in a very profound way. It blows my mind that I'd be in the position that I'm in right now. Each day has meaning and challenge. Thank you.

54. I'm thankful for a team that is flexible, willing to help one another, and willing to dive in and figure things out. We couldn't move forward without that attitude.

55. I'm thankful for ice cream. Most flavors are good, but cookie dough and cookies-and-cream take the cake.

56. I'm thankful for a husband who's willing to come out and rescue his gal, who happened to run out of gas during a major storm where all gas stations were closed because of a power outage. That's my man.

57. I'm thankful for backup power; without it, we could not have contacted our members who were participating in our webcast when all the power went out and the video feed was lost. Thank you for small contingencies.

58. I'm thankful for powdered brownies. Oh, what a treat.

59. I'm thankful for God's patience and calmness filling me today as I dealt with all the issues presented by today's storms. I never felt stressed or on edge. Thank you.

60. I'm thankful for the confirmation that God has given me regarding my writing and my book. It's been so difficult to bring this book (*The Power of Rest*) to market that it'd be easy to get discouraged, but God keeps sending me that little jolt I need to keep going.

61. I'm thankful for having a medicine ball that I can use to stretch out my back. I don't know why my back stiffens as it does. Perhaps it's just age. But whatever the reason, time spent stretching on the medicine ball does the trick.

62. I'm thankful for Honey Nut Cheerios and other healthy, flavorful cereal. I don't have to load myself up with sugar to have a tasty breakfast or snack.

63. I'm thankful for our local library. I'm able to make progress on my reading list while controlling spending because of our incredible library system. I enjoy going there and picking up two to three books at a time. This frees me to use my budget to buy books that I want to continue to have as reference material in the years to come.

64. I'm thankful for Patrick McBane and Transformational Leadership. It's a privilege to be involved in bringing this ministry to Columbus.

65. I'm thankful for John Scroggins and The Baton Exchange. It's a privilege to have some role in investing in our young adults as they enter into the marketplace.

66. I'm thankful for quiet Sunday afternoons where I can reflect on the nature of God, invest in my development and the development of others, and prepare myself for the upcoming week.

67. I'm thankful for pastors who have decided to put pen to paper and share their lives, learning with me through books. I've grown so much in my own walk because of those who have walked before me and passed along their notes.

68. I'm thankful that we are able to grow and change every moment of our lives. We are not stuck as we are as long as we're open to moving.

69. I'm thankful for the new women that are signing up for women ministry events. I'm excited about the opportunity to be a part of these ladies' lives.

70. I'm thankful for nativity scenes that dot my house in different places. They're a wonderful reminder of the incredible gift of life that you've given to us at such a significant price. You gave all so that we may be reconciled back to you. Thank You, Lord.

71. I'm thankful for cheerful coworkers. We spend so much time at work. How miserable it would be if the environment was negative. Thank You, Lord, for leading me to a place that is encouraging and positive.

72. I'm thankful for divine connections. So many different aspects of my life have intertwined after the past few years

that only God could have woven them together into this beautiful tapestry.

73. I'm thankful that I had an opportunity to lavish praise on someone whom I had to spend so much time challenging, pushing, and critiquing. And even better, the praise was done in a group setting, whereas the critiques have occurred in private just as it should be. Thank You, Lord, for that opportunity.

74. I'm thankful that I've been able to make plans with Dana for this weekend, even if they are cleaning related. We'll get to spend a little bit of time together doing something.

75. I'm thankful for the chance to learn about the spread of Christianity around the world. Though there is severe persecution, there is also exponential growth and a resurrected hope. Thank You, Lord, for calling people to go out to the mission field.

76. I'm thankful that I was able to resolve questions from our customers today.

77. I'm thankful that I've been placed under leaders who are truly qualified to lead.

78. I'm thankful I got to hear my coworker's heart today. Her passion was obvious.

79. I'm thankful for Tuesday morning prayer times at church. It's become a time of being able to really zero in on life and its purpose.

80. I'm thankful for the opportunity extended to me to attend a Bethel Worship Night.

81. I'm thankful that I have coworkers whom I can run things by and get input from. We have really good leaders from whom I can learn.

82. I'm thankful that I have women whom I can share my struggles with as I muddle through the complexities called my family.

83. I'm thankful that I'm working and doing life with people with a sense of humor. Life would be miserable without the gift of laughter.

84. I'm thankful for those who continue to push me to have the difficult conversations. I'm being forced out of my comfort zone in order to give others the support they need.

85. I'm thankful that God continues to work on my disposition. I can be temperamental, critical, and aloof when I forget what's important and start focusing on self. Thankfully I go into that state less often, and God draws me out of that state of being more quickly. I'm a work in process, but that's no excuse for me to continue in behaviors that I know are not acceptable.

86. I'm thankful that God has taken away all taste for alcohol. Despite the stressful day and resulting tension headache, I had zero longing for any alcoholic tonic. I was able to relax through natural means.

87. I'm thankful that my husband has become so self-sufficient. There was a time when I would have had to nag him to take care of things like renewing his license, but not anymore. He simply gets things done that he needs to get done. It's so much easier to step aside and let him lead.

88. I'm thankful for those who are able to see beyond and have called me out into ministry in unexpected ways.

89. I'm thankful that God continues to challenge me to go beyond myself. I can easily get complacent and rehash old accomplishments, but today's a new day.

90. I'm thankful that I'm able to enjoy the sunrise in the morning. My days are not so hectic that I can't take the time to appreciate the beauty that surrounds me.

I haven't added an entry into my gratitude journal since 2016. I find myself giving thanks every morning when I wake up and most evenings when I go to bed. I haven't found myself slipping into ungratefulness, and so I haven't taken the time to write additions to the journal. But if a time should come when I feel myself slipping back into a "woe is me" pride, then I will make entry 91 and will continue to make entries until I know that life disappointments are not settling into my soul and festering into disappointment. Should I not be able to push myself there, I know that I have friends, people I've chosen to do life with, who will push me there. Character formation happens in relationship. If you haven't surrounded yourself by people who will speak truth to you and encourage you to look outside yourself when you're becoming too whiny, then you're missing out on one of the best gifts that you can give to yourself.

ACCOUNTABILITY: A COUNTERMEASURE

Our path to greatness, though uniquely individualized, is not meant to be traveled alone. We are meant to travel alongside one another, encouraging at all times and admonishing when necessary. We are meant to speak loving truth when we see a person beginning to veer offtrack so that they may turn back onto the right path. We need the truth, as painful as it is to hear, spoken into us. We need a friend courageous enough to say that we're becoming self-centered and unbearable. We are to heed James 5:20 as it relates to helping to turn a sinner from the error of his ways.

We're not meant to be harsh or judgmental about it. We all make mistakes; we all face temptations. We're all subject to rationalization and compromise, though often in different areas based on our own unique personalities. Staying grounded in our frailties and in others' frailties is vital to staying on the right path. When we begin to think more highly of ourselves than we ought to, then we are setting the stage for a purpose-derailing detour. It's inevitable that we'll turn our thoughts inward.

If you've read this section and recognized yourself, don't despair. It's not difficult to stop the swerve and get back on course. It just requires intentionally choosing to turn back toward your original purpose and motives. We'll cover more on rerouting in the next section.

GROUP 2: ON THE WRONG PATH/IN NEED OF REROUTING

What if you missed the early warning signals and are squarely on the wrong path, is there a way to get back on the right path absent a crisis situation?

As I look at my own story, I'd have to answer that question with an emphatic yes. As a teenage mom, my primary driver and motivator was providing a good life for my son. I didn't need anything fancy; a roof over our heads, food on the table, and clothes on our backs were sufficient. I remember my very first car, a 1992 Chevy Cavalier. It wasn't exotic, but it was mine. I purchased it about a month after graduating college and starting my first job. It was the first thing that I had ever owned, and it was beautiful. Likewise, I still remember the excitement of buying was first house. It was a little starter house that cost all of $29,000. That may not sound like a lot of money, but that was a lot of money for someone whose income on her very first tax return was $5,349 from a job worked while in college. My beginnings were very humble indeed.

Fast-forward ten years to 2002. By then, I was well on my way to becoming a career-obsessed workaholic with a supermom syndrome. I was an up-and-coming business professional who also coached sports, served on a couple of nonprofit boards, cooked dinner almost every day, and actively participated in PTA and booster clubs. I gave my kids the extras I didn't have growing up, but I was still quite mindful of not spoiling them too much (at least at that time). They had nice toys but not necessarily the latest toys, nice clothes but not necessarily brand clothes, and a reasonable amount of spending money for trips to the store. They had chores to do and rules to follow. They joined me in my community service days. We picked up trash, visited with moms in homes for unwed mothers, read to the elderly, and enjoyed every minute of it as a family. Yes, I thought I could do it all and had life figured out; no one was going to prove me wrong. As my income increased, so did my lifestyle. Annual vacations became somewhat standard. I started spending more on myself—massages, salon appointments, and the like. It was no longer cool to have a home spa and do my own hair.

Fast-forward eight more years to 2010, eighteen years into my career. By this time, I had joined a private club where established and aspiring business leaders routinely networked over lunch or afternoon cocktails. I had settled into a routine of going to the theater several times a year with dinner at an upscale restaurant prior to a Broadway play. I had upgraded my wardrobe and accessories to better fit in with the movers and shakers with whom I more regularly came into contact. I also gave to charity regularly in amounts that I thought were generous. I was a United Way Key Club member and a founding member of the United Way's Women Leadership Council. I went to black-tie charity balls and participated in silent auctions. I did all the right things to be noticed and recognized in the community, and I was successful. I received numerous community awards and public recognition at several ceremonies. The purity of my motives back in 1992 had been thoroughly corrupted. My career was no longer about providing for my family—it had become a quest to make a name for myself. My charitable involvement was no longer about helping those who needed a hand because I was once one of them, understood how it felt, and wanted them to know that their circumstances didn't define them. It was no longer about them feeling like they were seen and loved. It had become about my name and reputation. I had detoured and was completely on the wrong path.

If a poll was taken in 2010, I'd been the least likely person to be picked to write a book on rest or on greatness. I was far away from both. In 2011, I would experience burnout and severe (suicidal-level) depression that would send me into a tailspin of self-destructive behaviors. I did not realize how far offtrack I was until these self-destructive behaviors almost cost me my freedom. I believe God allowed me to experience what I did because I wouldn't have pressed pause otherwise. With His loving, often firm, and sometimes painful correction, I was able to get back on track. It was in the midst of this corrective process that I realized that all that I had done, all that I had accomplished, and all that I had given meant nothing because it was all about me. My actions were not motivated by love. Though I continue to experience professional success and generate an income that allows me to provide a comfortable lifestyle for my family while giving generously, my outlook on life is very different. I give without people knowing that I'm giving. I serve without people knowing that I'm serving. I genuinely celebrate the successes of others. I'm comfortable leading from the position I'm in; I don't need promotions or greater prominence. I no longer use retail therapy or alcohol therapy to feel good. I don't need a full schedule to feel as if I'm doing something that matters. There are some who'd look at my life today and view it as less successful than before because my income is lower and I'm not in the public as much. I disagree. I'm far more successful today in my "average" life than I was before in my "glamorous" life.

So can you get back on the right path? No. It will be painful. It will cost you. You may have to let go of beliefs, relationships, career goals, material possessions, long-held dreams, and more as you go through a course correction. You may even feel like you're fading into obscurity as you exit the spotlight for a period of time, much like an exhibit that's taken off the display floor for reconstruction. In the beginning, you may be bothered by how quickly people move on. You may pine for the days when people sought you ought to ask for your opinion. You may even question your identity now that you've fallen off the public radar screen. But if you fully surrender to the process and trust it unfailingly, then you'll reach a point where these things will no longer matter. You'll emerge from the reconstruction firmly grounded and rooted in living out your life as a humble servant of the Most High God. You will be ready to lay down your life in service to others not for what you can get of it but because that's who you are. You will give of your time, talent, and treasures cheerfully and sacrificially because that's who you are. You will engage in life fully, enjoying all the blessings of God, which includes financial provision, but you won't be the least bit tempted to indulge in the excesses that mark our consumeristic society. You will take pleasure in pouring out blessings to your family and spending times of celebration with them because that's who you are. When all these things are true, you've discovered greatness. It may not look like the world's portrait of greatness. Your name may or may not be famous. You may start your own business, and it may become a multimillion-dollar organization, or it may hold steady as a solid small business employing just a few people. The outcome is not what's important; your faithful service in what you're uniquely created and called to do is what matters. You may write a book that only a few people read, or it may become a best seller—it doesn't matter. You may launch a technological innovation that changes life as we know it, or you may work diligently and faithfully for years without any breakthrough—it doesn't matter. You've been faithful, and that's what matters.

But how do you get started? All change starts the same way: with a decision. You must decide to change. No one can make this decision for you. I love my oldest son dearly. He was on the wrong path for ten years. As much as I loved him during that time, I couldn't force him onto the right path. I couldn't make that decision for him. He had to that for himself. And so must you.

Once that initial decision is made, then you must quickly take action to put the change in motion and surround yourself with the necessary support system to stay committed over the long haul. You cannot procrastinate or else rationalization will set in. The more your identity is threatened, the stronger the resistance will be. There's a reason why battered women return to their abusers seven times on average before leaving for good, and it's not because they enjoy abuse. Addicts don't return to their addictions because they love being in bondage and the havoc it wreaks on their lives and the lives of their loved ones. Offenders don't return to criminal activities because they hate society, want to hurt their families, or love jail. There's a stronger power at work. The character formation that needs to occur within them will only occur through blood, sweat, and tears. It may take years for that power to be broken. It's not broken easily, it's not broken alone, and it's not broken solely through man's efforts. And when it finally is broken, community will be paramount. A strong community is critical for those at the beginning stages of trying to reform their character. When people are in the midst of defining their new identity, understanding their purpose in life, and taking the initial steps to charting a new journey, they are vulnerable. A misstep here can have devastating consequences. It's so easy to fall backward at this stage, and each backward fall can make the next upward climb more difficult. Community provides the support necessary to stabilize a person during this stage. I would not be where I'm at today without my church community, and I don't mean the people I see on a Sunday, say a casual hello to, and then go on my way. I'm talking about the people who were there to help me slay the dragons.

Many books have been written on how to walk through life with people breaking free from life-controlling habits, I will not attempt to cover the complexities here. What matters for our purposes is the realization that the character formation process is just that, a process. It occurs over time and not all at once. It sometimes involves challenges that we must face if we are to progress. For those going through the character formation (or recreation) process and those supporting them during this process, it's important to know what these challenges look like so that we do not short-circuit character development. In our attempt to do good and be supportive, we can do great harm. We will visit that topic as we discuss the rerouting process (aka character formation or character recreation) as we look at our third group.

GROUP 3: IN THE MIDST OF THE REROUTING PROCESS

This may be one of the hardest groups to be in. I already mentioned that the rerouting process can be painful and that there's much that you may need to let go of in order to reroute. The process can also be time-consuming depending on how far offtrack you've veered. If you set out from Columbus, Ohio (my home) with the intention of going to Miami, Florida, but suddenly found yourself in Topeka, Kansas (720 miles west), there's no way for you to get back on track except to turnaround and backtrack for a few hundred miles until you can reroute onto a highway that will take you to Miami. It's not the same highway you would've taken if you had set out from Columbus, but it will still get you there. The journey from Columbus to Miami would've taken you 17 hours, whereas the journey from Topeka to Miami will take you 21 hours. And you would have traveled for roughly 10.5 hours to get to Topeka.

Now, if you didn't happen to notice that you we're going the wrong way until you reached Albuquerque, New Mexico, you would've veered 1,456 miles offtrack and traveled for 21 hours in the wrong direction. The distance you have to travel to get back on track is much greater than the person who turned around in Topeka.

Conceptually I think we get this idea, but that doesn't mean that we like how it feels when we're experiencing it as a reality in our lives. The pain of correction can lead us to abort the process. It's easy to stop short of our destination and settle at a midway point. We get weary, see a pleasant spot, and stop. It may not be exactly where we're supposed to be, but it's good enough. It's still a far distance from where we came from, we rationalize. We may even take pride in our ability to flex and go with the flow. However, we must guard against that tendency. Our intended destinies can only be achieved if we keep going.

If you've ever had a wart, you know how painful it can be when multiple layers of dead skin cover it and pressure is applied. When that pain is in full force, you'd do anything to get rid of it—until that pain is lessened to the point of being bearable. Then the thought of enduring the searing pain of core removal weakens your resolve. We know that removing the core is the only way to guarantee that the wart doesn't come back, but it hurts a lot. Why not just keep removing the dead skin that grows over it? It's not ideal, but you can live with it. That's what it's like to abort the rerouting process. You stop short of ever reaching the destination because you don't want to deal with the pain of extracting the core, and so you settle for a less-than-perfect solution. You abort the character-development process and never reach the full measure of greatness that was intended for you.

Never was I more tempted to settle than when it came to confronting the sexual abuse I endured during my tween years. I convinced myself that I had made peace with my past, so there was no reason to resurrect those painful memories. I had forgiven all involved, including myself, as it relates to the subsequent decisions I made throughout my teenage years. I had acknowledged the negative influence it had on my marriage and had worked through those issues. I was back on track personally and professionally. What was to be gained by opening those wounds anew? Yet, he thought kept coming to me that I wasn't yet at the core, and unless I wanted it to be like a wart, I had to keep going. I wasn't whole yet. How could that be? It's at this point in your journey where your guides require great discernment. It would've been easy for my friends to discourage me from going any further. They could've supported my rationalization and encouraged me to stay where I was at, but they didn't. They were sympathetic to my pain but also understood that personal growth was on the other side of that pain, and therefore they allowed me to enter into the struggle.

Despite my inner resistance, I dug in. To my surprise, I found deep-rooted issues with trusting male authorities. These issues were at the heart of my staunch feminism. My value system had become distorted. Had I not dug deeper, I wouldn't have the rich relationships that I now have with male marketplace leaders. I wouldn't have been able to come alongside male church leaders and support their ministries. I would still be stuck—in a better place than where I was, but not at all where I was supposed to be and many people wouldn't have noticed the difference. I never would've been called out for aborting the process of my own character development. In fact, I would likely have been celebrated for my staunch support of women in leadership. The position I take now is not nearly as popular: one of coleadership. I'm not interested in women taking over the world, just in them realizing their God-given purpose. I am deeply concerned about the neglect of leadership development programs for our boys and young men. Their leadership is to be desired, not criticized and stigmatized. But I couldn't have gotten to this healthier point of view had I stopped.

So how do you prevent yourself from aborting the process? How do you make sure that you don't settle for halfway? It's easy to say endure the pain knowing that there's reward on the other side of that pain, but how do you actually do so in reality? Is there a secret to making it through?

Every path is different. Every journey is unique. But, just like completing a marathon, they all require discipline. There will be times when you have to dig in and persevere. Weariness may have seeped into your mind, body, and soul, but you have to keep going. You'll want to do more than rest—you'll want to quit. Still, you have to keep going. Just like I had to tell myself to keep going during the half marathon, you have to tell yourself to take the next step, then the next step, and then the next step. You cannot focus on how many more miles there are to go, or you will be discouraged. You will begin to wonder whether you have enough energy in your tank to make it to the end (you probably don't). You will begin to wonder whether the effort is worth it (it is). You'll begin to wonder whether you'd be better off quitting now and celebrating your victory (you're not). There's no secret to making it through. It all comes down to reconnecting with God, engaging in a strong faith community, consistent practice of spiritual disciplines, and good old-fashioned mental resolve. The battlefield is in your mind, soul, and spirit. You cannot when such a battle using the weapons that the world likes to deploy. You win a spiritual battle with spiritual tools. These include prayer, reading of scripture, and participating in a faith community. You need others on the battlefield with you. This is not a battle you want to fight alone—you will lose. However, with the right support group, you will win that battle and will get back on track. The process could take years, but you will get there.

GROUP 4: BACK ON TRACK/DON'T WANT TO DETOUR AGAIN

If you, like me, have gotten back on track and want to be sure to never detour again, how do you guard yourself?

First, you need to learn from your journey through reflection and introspection. Resist the temptation to rush this process, to bury the pain of the past and move forward. Reflect upon the situation. How did you get there? What decisions did you make? Why did you make them? How were others affected? But don't stop there. Engage in a healthy dose of introspection over a period of time. What beliefs were at work within the decisions you made? What did you belief to be true about yourself, about others, and about the world? How will those beliefs need to change for you to stay on the right path? What values might you need to change? What social networks may need to change? What habits might you need to change? Introspection should cause you to ask the difficult questions. Am I really willing to pay the cost of walking on this path? How committed am I to change? What will I do when I'm tempted? During this stage of your journey, solitude is your friend. Solitude gives you the space you need to thoroughly examine your life. Solitude doesn't require long periods spent away from the world, though, when you have time to get away you should. Solitude may simply mean taking a long walk on a Saturday morning. Or solitude may mean getting up a little earlier in the morning a spending an hour in quietness with a journal at hand. The key is to eliminate the external and internal distractions. Whatever that looks like for you, that's what solitude means. Once you've done this introspection, you're ready to take the next step.

Earlier, I mentioned guardrails as a tool to prevent you from detour. Well, they are just as effective at preventing you from detouring a second time once you're back on track. Use your introspection to determine what guardrails you need. The first three months after I decided to stop drinking alcohol were incredibly difficult for me. I was surprised by how many invitations to wine tastings and happy hours I received. I don't believe the volume suddenly increased; I was simply much more alert to them because I knew that I couldn't attend them—at least, not at that time while I was making such a pivotal change in habits. Some Friday evenings, I attended Celebrate Recovery. I didn't feel that I needed the whole program, however it gave me something to do on a Friday evening that didn't involve going to a bar to listen to a band play. It also gave me the opportunity to publicly proclaim to myself and to others the new lifestyle I had committed myself to live. I needed that declaration, especially during the holiday season when alcohol flows pretty freely at family gatherings. I couldn't begin to count how many times I was offered a drink within my first hour of being at a business networking event or upon arriving home for the holidays. Fast-forward to today. Now, I can attend business-related happy hours and wine tasting, family celebrations, and other alcohol-laden activities without even a hint of temptation. I have zero desire for alcoholic beverages.

The guardrails that I need today are not the same as the ones I needed at the beginning of my change, because the temptations have changed. You can't tempt me with alcohol, but a venti decaf, sugar-free vanilla latte with soy, almond, or coconut milk? Now we're talking. At a cost of $5.25 per drink, if you're buying, I will meet you at the coffee bar. I hope you see through this that change is possible. Is it easy? No. The concepts themselves are very simple, and there's nothing complicated within this book. However, simple does not equate to easy. The concept of weight loss is simple: you consume fewer calories than you burn. But weight loss is a struggle for many—conceptually simple but not easy. And so it with achieving greatness. The concept is simple: allow God to shape you into a person of holy character. But the execution is not easy. If you're to have any hope of success, you must catch a vision for change.

CHAPTER 8

CATCHING A VISION

Intentional change always starts with a vision. Hopefully as you've read this book, you were able to catch a vision of the mind-set, attitudes, and behaviors of a truly great person, and you can see yourself in that image. I don't need to know you personally to know that greatness lies within you; it's inherent in your makeup. I don't need to know your story to know that greatness is still within your reach regardless of the valleys through which you may have tread, the detours you may have taken, or the length of time you've been offtrack. Greatness has always been and will always be your destiny, and restoration has always been and will always be available.

You don't need to know your ultimate path to greatness to get started. You simply need to focus on the mind-set, attitudes, and behaviors that will position you for success. I hope that you've been able to identify which attributes you possess and which ones you may lack. If you have, then you've established the foundation for creating a vision of where you want to be one year from now. It's now time to take the vision to the next level by answering these five questions.

1. How do you want people to experience you? Or said another way, how do you want them to feel when in your company and after you leave?

_____

_____

_____

_____

_____

2. What adjectives do you want people to use to describe your nature or character?

_____

_____

_____

_____

_____

3. What images do you want people to conjure up when they think of you and try to describe to others what it's like to be around you?

_____

_____

_____

_____

_____

4. What do you want to be celebrated for one year from now?

_____

_____

_____

_____

_____

5. What would greatness look like in your life based on your talents, abilities, and resources?

_____

_____

_____

_____

_____

As tempting as it may be to jot down a few words and move on, resist that urge. Take the time to do some serious reflection on each of these five questions because they are going to become your guiding compass as you move forward. Once you've answered these five questions, then it's time to convert those answers into vision and mission statements. Although we often refer to vision and mission statements in the same breadth and interchangeably, they are not the same. Vision statements are aspirational and inspirational. They reflect where you're headed. Mission statements are about the present day. They reflect why you do what you do. To put these into perspective, I've included my own vision and mission statements as examples.

My vision statement:

I will empower leaders to become disciple makers so that the love of God is manifested and the glory of His power is released to do its transformational work resulting in radiant, abundant, and unified living.

My mission statement:

Develop meaningful relationships with my family, my church, my community, and the leaders who direct them so that I'm able to speak truth and encouragement into their lives.

Once you've converted the answers to your five questions into a rough vision and mission statement, then it's time for you to dig just a little deeper. It's time for you to look at who you are right now. Take a few minutes to answer these three questions.

1. **What are you so passionate about that it consumes your time and attention?** This is the topic that you're constantly reading about, the hobby that you can't step away from, or the cause that compels you into action. For me, it's people. I love to study human behavior—how me make decisions, how

we form groups and teams, how we learn, and how we relate to one another, to God, and to our world. I enjoy hearing, reading about, and generally studying people's stories of trials and triumphs. I want to see people succeed and fulfill their life's calling; it's what gets me out of bed every day. I cringe internally, and sometimes externally, whenever I hear a person demean another person, especially if that person is in a place of influence or authority over the person being demeaned. Tears flow freely when I encounter a person with shrunken shoulders and a wilted spirit because they've been so beat down by life. I would give almost anything to see their confidence and hope restored. Developing leaders is not about growing wealthy or selling leadership how-to books. For me, developing leaders is paramount to helping individuals realize their destiny.

2. **What would people say about you if your funeral was tomorrow?** In essence, how are people currently experiencing you? There was a time when my family would've mentioned my work or my career success. But I came to a point where I realized that I didn't care whether people thought of me as accomplished. I did care whether they had experienced my love, kindness, and compassion. I didn't care if they had ever read one of my books or sat in one of my classes, but I did care whether they felt like I've regularly encouraged, challenged, and valued them. I wanted them to have felt like my presence was comforting and reassuring. I wanted them to have felt listened to and cherished. I wanted them to feel like their lives were made better for me having been a part of it. So I changed my focus. I became more focused on manifesting the love of God in and through me. I began to see that my life as a leader was about displaying the only true source of unadulterated, unconditional, and unshakeable goodness. And so my vision statement changed.

3. **What talents and abilities stand out?** There may be lots of things that you are good at, but what is that you are great at? What seems to come so naturally to you that others routinely call it out? My daughter has a way of interacting with children that amazes me every time I see it in action. Kids flock to her and respond to her in a way that they don't with me. This gifting, combined with several other gifts (including athleticism, linguistic acquisition, and creative artistry), makes ministering to children a breeze to her. I could formally study for years and not be able to create programs that she's able to create without training. It would make no sense for me to have a vision statement that is centered on kids when my talents and abilities best equip me to work with adults. I could've saved myself many years of unfruitful volunteer work if I had come to this reality sooner. I wouldn't have spent so much time trying to conjure up an affinity for children-related community service opportunities.

As you answer these three questions, it's imperative that you don't answer them based on what others would expect of you. For women whose lives have been defined by their roles as daughters, wives, mothers, homemakers, and caregivers, answering these three questions objectively can be very difficult. I can't even begin to count how many women I've interacted with who state that they have no marketable skills or limited talents and abilities because they've only ever been stay-at-home moms. They don't see any greatness within them. To which I say hogwash. A stay-at-home mom is the ultimate organizer, negotiator, and peacemaker. She's a logistical expert, financial planner, and part-time nurse. The list could go on. But beyond all of these "skills" lies a heart of service, sacrifice, love, kindness, gentleness, and compassion. She has the key attributes to success in life brewing in her often completely under her radar screen. All she really needs is someone to come along and help her see the value the she already contributes and the greatness that already resides with her. The significance that can seem beyond her grasp is right there, unseen and unspoken of by a society that values pedigrees, positions, accomplishments, and wealth. Having this balanced view can help draft a vision and mission statement that truly reflects God's unique plan versus being reactive to or rebellious toward expectations.

Similarly, men often struggle with expectations of being extroverted, competitive, and highly driven toward goal accomplishment. Talents and abilities that fall more on the nurturing side could be discounted or ignored within the context of creating a vision statement because they don't "conform" to the norm. But last I checked, men tended to the needs of the widows in the church, including distribution of food and prayer, and this wasn't considered soft or unmacho. Serving others wasn't a command given to women alone. Being the least and putting others ahead of yourself didn't seem to be "bad" goals. So don't allow the world's distortion of manhood shape what greatness means to you in terms of your own mission and vision statement. Allow your plan to reflect God's unique design for you whatever that looks like.

Young adults, don't worry if you're vision statement is too ambitious for some people. It's not for them; it's for you. Older adults, don't worry if your vision statement seems too unrealistic for some people. It's not for them; it's for you. Age is not a relevant consideration factor when establishing your vision statement. Don't worry if your vision statement doesn't seem to fit your current circumstances. Where you're at currently in life is not a good indicator of where you're going, especially if you've been meandering through life. The only true measure of a good vision statement is whether it reflects the destiny which God has designed specifically for you. It's only within that destiny that you will find true greatness; no other vision will get you to the goal.

Don't concern yourself with crafting the perfect vision statement because you'll refine it over time as you get better at listening to

God's voice. Your initial vision statement is merely a starting point for you. It's the big-picture view of your life message. It provides the guardrails within which you can begin to evaluate existing commitments and new opportunities, and it's the guidepost against which you can track your journey. But it is not a plan. Plans have details; a vision statement does not. Your vision statement is like your skeletal structure: everything hangs off of it. When it's out of alignment, your body pays for it, though you may not realize that's the issue. The pain in your knee may result from an issue in your back. That's how powerful vision is in our lives. When our vision is askew, our lives are out of whack, but we may not realize the underlying cause, and so we often do like we do with a physical pain: we treat the symptoms. However, the symptoms reoccur. Don't make the mistake here. Don't rush the process of crafting your vision statement. Be willing to draft it and redraft it until it feels right. Only after you feel you're there with your vision statement should you move to the next stage, defining your strategies.

Your strategic plan is like your muscular system. It fills in your shape and allows you to move with purpose. It will narrow the focus of your vision statement, defining both who and how. There are many ways that I could develop people and many different people groups I could focus on developing. I'm not called to develop everyone; that's an impossible task. I'm called to focus in on certain groups of people in very specific ways that fit my talents and abilities. I've divided my strategic plan into two focus areas: developing and leading self and developing and leading marketplace leaders. Within each focus area, I've defined key objectives with a limit of five for any category.

1. Developing and Leading Self
   a. Holistically healthy lifestyle
   b. Healthy family life
   c. Healthy relationships
   d. Healthy marketplace leadership
   e. Healthy church

2. Developing and Leading Marketplace Leaders
   a. Equipping existing marketplace leaders
   b. Mobilizing and connecting church and marketplace
   c. Mobilizing marketplace leaders to deploy compassion ministries in underserved areas of need

Though all of these objectives have actions associated with them, they're not necessarily independent from one another. For example, some of the actions I take to model healthy marketplace leadership also help me with equipping existing marketplace leaders. It's not a one-to-one relationship. The simplicity of having eight objectives that shape where I invest my time did not develop overnight. When I first started this process, I had a long list of objectives, but over time with much prayer and reflection, I was able to discern what needed to be the driving forces for my life. The value of this simplicity cannot be overstated. I'm presented with many opportunities to volunteer my time and give of my resources. This framework has helped me to stay focused so that I'm swimming in the lane I was meant to swim in. I interact with a lot of individuals who are doing great things, and it would be easy to engage in comparison and come away feeling inadequate and insignificant. This framework has helped me nurture contentment because I'm able to come back to it and realize that I'm right where I'm supposed to be, and that is the essence of a successful life. I'm often confronted by opportunities to do things my way, which can be appealing to someone who prefers to have results yesterday. However, this framework anchors me and keeps me centered on outcomes. I know that the outcomes I want can only be achieved over time through a process, and so I'm able to wait.

As I've walked out my vision statement with its supporting strategies, I've had to change my philanthropic giving, unwind commitments, sever old alliances, and form new ones. Many of those changes were painful. I was pulling money or time away from an organization, and that's never easy. I was ending relationships with people I cared about, and it hurt. But I was offtrack and had to ask myself whether

I was willing to endure the pain and weather the grief of getting back on track. Looking back, I don't regret those decisions, as painful as they were at the time.

Once you have your vision statement and supporting strategies, you need to use it. Make it a habit to review this vision statement and supporting strategies at least quarterly so that it becomes a part of how you think about yourself and your life. You cannot just leave it sitting in a notebook. You need to become intentional about it, meditate over it, pray about it, and allow God to convict you of behaviors, attitudes, and actions that are inconsistent with it. Take ownership of the person you are to become. Speak into that person. And most important, give yourself grace. Remember that you are on a journey. You're on a journey to become the great person that God always intended you to be. On that journey, you will make mistakes. You will fail. You will have moments where you don't live up to the vision of who you are to be, who God designed you to be. That's okay.

When failure happens—and it will—acknowledge it. Confess it. Allow God to show you why you failed and release it over to God to work with it. Learn from it. Return back to your vision statement. Recommit to it and move forward. A life of character, a life of destiny, a life of greatness is forged a moment at a time over many years. It doesn't happen in a day. It doesn't happen in a week. It doesn't happen in a year. If you're going to achieve a greatness that matters, you'll need to commit for the long haul. You're running a long-distance race where the manner in which you run, and how well you finish the race, matters just as much as crossing the finish line. No matter how enticing it may be, don't fall for a shortcut that promises all the rewards with little or none of the work. Don't detour off course; stay focused on the race God intended for you to run. Your great destiny awaits you.

APPENDIX 1

LEADERSHIP CHARACTERISTICS
AS DEFINED IN THE BOOK

Leadership is not a title; it's influence. As you pursue your life of greatness, you will have the opportunity to influence many people. Submitting to the character formation process will establish you firmly within the leadership traits that matter. "What character traits are those?" you may ask. Let me tell you—or rather, let me point you to the authoritative source. Thousands of books are written on leadership every year. Leadership training is a multibillion-dollar business. Debates rage over the definition of leadership, the most important leadership characteristics, and the effectiveness of different leadership styles. Given how much energy goes into debating leadership development, you'd think an authoritative source on desirable leadership traits was lacking; nothing could be further from the truth. If we want to get to the heart of leadership, we need go no further than the Bible itself. Regardless of whether you believe in the Bible's divine authorship, inerrancy, or authority, you cannot deny the wisdom contained within it as it pertains to leadership.

From the Bible, we clearly see that leadership is an attitude. It's a way of thinking that impacts how we live, how we communicate, and how we associate with others. Sound leadership recognizes the concept of stewardship. Leaders understand that the status of leader comes with responsibilities and accountability. We are granted authority not to indulge our selfish desires but to enable us to discharge our leadership responsibilities for the good of those we lead. That's why if you are going to be a leader, you have to start with how you think about yourself and the purpose for the authority that you have as a leader. From there, you have to dive into the four key aspects of leadership—values and principles, communication, collaboration, and accountability—that are the hallmark of great leaders everywhere.

As we look at leadership in the Bible, we also see there is a stark difference between worldly authority and biblical authority. Worldly authority is derived from the power and influence that you are able to wield over other people. Wealth and armory often convey this authority. This type of authority is unevenly distributed. Leadership based on worldly authority is easily corrupted as people fear its loss. Compromise often becomes the only way to hold onto this authority. Biblical authority is based on destiny. It's intended to accomplish a purpose, to get a job done. So when we're given authority, we need to ask ourselves some questions.

1. Why were we given this authority (expressed purpose)?
2. Given that purpose, how are we to use this authority within our current context (practical application)?
3. What decisions must we make to carry out our designed purpose (responsibility)?
4. What haven't we taken authority over that is within our responsibility (neglect)?

Because we have this authority, we have the responsibility to act. We must guard ourselves against the tendency to shirk responsibility under the mistaken belief that someone else is taken care of it. What is ours to do is ours to do. It's part of our journey to greatness. Abdication is not allowed. When we look at Moses, King David, and Paul, we clearly see leaders who took responsibility and used their authority to lead their people. It doesn't mean they were perfect, as we will also see, but they did work toward their purpose. Samson, King Saul, and Xerxes stand is stark contrast. These leaders didn't under the source or purpose for the authority that they had and did not use it appropriately.

LEADERSHIP LESSONS FROM MOSES, KING DAVID, AND PAUL

Moses had a difficult mission: he needed to lead a ragtag group of former slaves to a new home and transform them into a self-governing nation along the journey. He faced the ultimate organizational challenge in a rather unforgiving environment with ungrateful people. King David was the second in line of the kings of Israel. He had to lead during a time of war, when Israel was not securely planted in the land they called home. Paul had to lead during the early years of the Christian Church, when persecution was severe and the culture was immoral and self-indulgent. He had to teach people how to live a life of holiness in the midst of a pagan culture. From examining their leadership, we can learn a few key lessons.

1. Leaders worth emulating are developed over time. David's character forged out in the field, as a shepherd tending to flock. It was further refined during his time of serving for and then running from King Saul. Long before David actually carried the official title of king, the qualities that were going to shape his kingship were being formed.

2. Leaders who reach their destinies are teachable. The demands of leadership commanded every ounce of Moses's energy and time, and there were still decisions left unmade and needs

unmet. Moses had to learn to delegate to an appointed leadership team. He had to empower them to handle everyday matters while he attended to the more strategic issues. But had he not been willing to listen to the counsel of his father-in-law, Jethro, he may not have learned this lesson and the people would've suffered. David sought out counsel on battle strategies and listened to the admonishment of his army chief and of the prophets when they confronted him about poor decisions he had made. Paul had to be taught the ways of Christianity after his conversion. He had to learn how to reframe his thinking.

3. Leaders overcome through persistence, patience, and resiliency. The Israeli people tested Moses on a regular basis. He had plenty of opportunities to quit and return to his former life as people grumbled, complained, and questioned him as a leader. Despite his emotional and physical exertion on a daily basis, he was still under attack by the very people for which he had sacrificed everything. If he was motivated by fame or power or loyalty, he would not have persevered through all the trials. David endured the ridicule of his brothers, the persecution of King Saul, and a bitter contesting of his right to kingship. Paul endured beatings, jail time, shipwrecks, betrayals, and abandonment as he traveled the region sharing the gospel. He traveled more miles in a day without the aid of modern transportation than today's average person. He instructed people on the same matters over and over again as they sought him ought to understand the Christian life. He could've given up on the Ephesians, Colossians, Galatians, Philippians, or Romans, but he didn't.

4. Leaders cast an enduring vision and equip others to carry out the vision. Moses routinely cast vision with the people as he relayed the instruction or commandments he received from God. He constantly reminded them who God was, who they

were in relationship to God, and the promises that God had made concerning them. David cast a vision for a temple, took steps to secure the required resources, and then passed the vision along to Solomon to bring to fruition. Paul cast vision for the early Church in his many letters to them.

5. Leaders set expectations. Despite the demands of organizing a new nation and living in the wilderness, Moses was expected to observe the Sabbath and teach the people to do the same. They were to rely on God and not themselves to provide what was needed so that they could observe the Sabbath. Moses had to establish this expectation with the people. Similarly, Paul routinely set expectations for behavior both through how he lived his life and through what he communicated in writing.

6. Leaders use their influence for good. Moses routinely interceded for the Israelite people. He saw himself as their shepherd and acting accordingly. David used his position as king to continue to forge a future for the Israeli nation. Paul used his Roman citizenship to continue to spread the gospel.

7. Leaders love the people they lead. Paul was able to put himself in a position to be heard because he was a student of the culture of the people he was called to lead. He used his understanding of Gentile culture to communicate truths to them using concepts with which they were familiar.

None of these leaders were without faults. All of them detoured from their destiny at some point. Moses murdered an Egyptian, fled into the desert, and provided an exhaustive list of why he was not qualified to go back to Egypt to lead his people out. He sometimes got angry with the people and acted in haste. David slept with another man's wife and then had him murdered in war to cover up the act and the resultant pregnancy. Paul ruthlessly and relentlessly persecuted

Christians. He approved of stoning Stephen to death. He dragged people out of their homes to take them to jail for their faith. After becoming a Christian, he had such a heated disagreement with Barnabas—the very person who vouched for his trustworthiness and mentored him—that they parted ways. Yet these individuals achieved the greatness that was intended for them. They didn't become so prideful that they weren't able to be humbled. They were able to be restored back onto their path.

LEADERSHIP LESSONS FROM SAMSON, KING SAUL, AND KING XERXES

Samson had a destiny that never fully materialized. He had been set apart from before birth to yield authority for a particular purpose. To reach that destiny, he needed to live a particular lifestyle. As long as his parents were responsible for him, he stayed on track toward his destiny. They observed the restrictions that were in place. As Samson grew, he encountered situations that would test his commitment to his destiny. They were character-defining moments for him. Would he honor the requirements of his leadership destiny? Would he continue to set himself apart? Time and time again, we see that the answer is no. Samson lusts after and ultimately marries a non-Israelite. He eats from the carcass of a dead animal. He murders individuals to settle a bet. He visits harlots. His moral compromises are many and ultimately lead to his downfall. His destiny is aborted.

Saul was appointed to be Israel's first king. He didn't seek out the kingship. In fact, he hid himself in baggage so as to not be found when it was time to announce him as king. He had to be pulled out of the baggage and brought in front of the people to be anointed as king. Clearly, pride had not yet taken hold, but it would. He started out well. A successful journey would mean an enduring kingship. His only responsibilities: comply with established restrictions and honor the commandments as he fulfilled the requirements of king.

He had a destiny. But his destiny would never fully materialize. The kingship would not pass down to his son or stay within his family line. It would be wrestled away from him as he veered off course. He decided to violate the restrictions placed upon king out of fear of losing the respect and loyalty of his people. He decided to keep that which he was commanded not to keep for the same reason. His insecurities turned him toward a self-focus. Him image mattered more than his character.

King Xerxes had some big shoes to fill after what King Cyrus and King Darius I had accomplished. His reputation was on the line as he ascended to the throne. Could his greatness possibly exceed that of those who came before him? Could he expand the kingdom by conquering Greece, a feat Darius I couldn't accomplish? Pride and insecurity began to consume Xerxes early on. He displayed his wealth for a full six months, followed by a seven-day banquet. What, other than pride, prompted his need to show off his kingdom for 180 days? There was also a strategy at work. He wanted to entice kings to join his expedition to Greece. He was trying to increase his military might. He needed a clear show of his strength and power. Displaying his wealth should've been enough, but it wasn't. At least, it wasn't for him. Seven days into the banquet, Xerxes still felt a need to display his greatness. He decided that Vashti would do just that. Vashti was a crown jewel. He didn't expect rebellion. His pride couldn't suffer that; he was showing his strength. So he deposed her.

While this great display and celebration went on, the city continued to function. People went hungry and were enslaved to make ends meet. Xerxes' indulgences were well-known throughout the kingdom. What type of respect do you think this garnered by the people? But Xerxes didn't care. Xerxes was not a people-centered leader—that much is clear. His orders (or edicts) were followed not out of respect but out of fear, and he was okay with that. Failure to submit to the king's order meant death to you and possibly your family, and he was okay with that. Whatever Xerxes wanted, he took. When he wanted a wife, the young ladies of the city were gathered together, selected based on their beauty, and then given a year of beauty treatments to further enhance their appeal. When he took a wife, she became his property. She was given the best of everything but couldn't approach her husband uninvited. To approach Xerxes without an invitation meant death unless he intervened. Everything about Xerxes' leadership reflects self-centeredness. Yet Xerxes had a destiny. He was intended for greatness. He had an incredible opportunity to build upon what King Cyrus and King Darius I had done for Israel. Ultimately he would, but not of his own volition. His prompting would come through Esther.

As self-centered as Xerxes was, he did have one redeeming quality: he valued the advice of his council. He did not consider himself an expert on everything, though he was the chosen leader. Additionally, setting aside times when his judgment was clouded by wine or his ego was threatened, Xerxes didn't just act on what was reported to him. Instead, he investigated reports and confirmed them as true. Likewise, the counsel of his advisers was less biased when Xerxes' pride wasn't on the line. Xerxes was most on track to reach his destiny when he wasn't caught up in making a name for himself. Sadly, those moments were rare. His pride wouldn't let him abandon Greece as a conquest. His pride allowed him to sign an edict that would wipe out an entire people group. That same pride would compel him to have Haman (and his sons) hanged for plotting the destruction of the Jews, and he'd authorize an edict that allowed the Jews to rise up and defend themselves against those who had intended to destroy them. In the end, Xerxes participated in the rescue of the Jews, but he could have accomplished so much more. His destiny never fully materialized.

There are many other examples I could've used in this section. Diverting from our destiny is easy to do as societal values tug at us, pulling us toward a self-centered focus. The self-centeredness of today may look different than that of yesterday. Historical leaders of biblical times weren't chasing likes or shares. They weren't able to go live on Facebook to film themselves doing random acts of kindness (which misses the point, by the way). They couldn't create documentaries of their philanthropic acts with hopes of going viral. So it looks different, but it's still the same issue: a pursuit of greatness based on achievement of power, position, or great feats.

LEADERSHIP LESSONS FROM PROVERBS

Proverbs 11 and 12 have a lot to say about the character of a leader. In Proverbs 11, we see that godly leaders display the following attributes.

- Integrity. We are to conduct transactions with honesty or, as scripture notes, with a just weight. Those who do business with us should never have a valid reason for believing they've been taken advantage of or that our motives are less than honorable.

- Humility. We are to reflect wisdom in our interactions with others. Wisdom demands that we think rightly of ourselves and of others. We don't exalt ourselves onto a pedestal, but we also don't debase ourselves.

- Righteousness. We value people and position our dealings from a foundation of relationship first.

- Discretion. We know when, what, and how to speak. We're able to control our tongues. We don't engage in gossip or idle conversation. We appreciate silence and use it wisely.

- Trustworthiness. We don't betray confidences or otherwise seek to inappropriately use confidential or sensitive information.

- Collaboration. We share information and seek guidance and advice from qualified individuals.

- Honor. We are to recognize the contributions of others. We're to praise that which is praiseworthy and conduct ourselves in ways that are honorable.

- Mercy. We do good to others and for others, even when we don't stand to benefit and when the recipients are not deserving of it.

- Steadfastness. We are persistent in living out our vision and values. We press through difficulties, holding steady to the course despite the obstacles that present themselves.

- Generosity. We are generous with recognition and with investing in people's personal goals and dreams. We are genuinely interested in their success and willing to invest our time, talent, and treasure in helping them succeed.

Proverbs 12 further expounds upon godly leaders. In this scripture, we say that godly leaders also display these characteristics.

- Teachable. We recognize the limits of our knowledge and our weaknesses. We not only are open to feedback but also seek it out and respond to it appropriately when given.

- Good reputation. We are consistent in the values that we display such that our reputation precedes us. We are known to be righteous and upright.

- Good thinkers. We have trained our mind to discern right and wrong. We seek just answers and not only easy, convenient answers.

- Diligent. We are hard-working and disciplined in our focus. We are able to get the work done that needs to get done.

- Prudent. We are not prone to acting irrationally out of emotional swings. Instead, we take the time to think through our actions before proceeding.

- Compassionate. We are moved by the suffering and conditions of others.

- Peaceful and joyous. We are calm in the midst of storms and joyful, even when operating in stressful, difficult situations. We seek to bring resolution and make peace because we value people and understand that conflict, left unaddressed, can damage the relationship and compromise success.

These noble traits are easily distorted. Good intentions can go astray. Humility, generosity, and compassion can become sources of pride. Pursuing a good reputation can become a means to an end. The quest for righteousness and prudence can morph into a judgmental and critical spirit. We can avoid conflict and rationalize it as maintaining peace and joy. Diligence can lead us to believe that we're entitled to a certain amount of rewards for our hard work. Staying on the right path isn't easy, but it is possible. Many others have graced the path, so we can too. The diagnosis is simple: exercise daily discipline in your thought life. Your heart will follow suit. Eventually, your actions will change to reflect your new mind-set. Stay alert and centered in your strengths while ever mindful of your weaknesses. Know the early warning signals that will caution you of impending danger. Respect those guardrails. Don't ignore them or rationalize them away. They're there for your protection. Expect discipline to become harder as your material success increases and your platform grows.

APPENDIX 2

CHARTING YOUR JOURNEY

Which picture do you visualize when you think about your personal journey?

Are you standing on the shore and looking out over the horizon, mesmerized by the vibrant reds, oranges, and purples splashed across the sky as dusk gives way to dark? Or are you staring out at a pitch-dark, starless sky devoid of any signs of life?

Do you expect smooth sailing on crystal clear waters, or do you expect choppy waters to materialize at random times as storms manifest? Do you see a steep mountain with rough terrain and limited shade, or a series of mountains with lush valleys separating them?

Our view of our journey is often colored by our current circumstances and our expectations of the future. If we're in a season of pain and struggle, it's hard to imagine anything good originating from our suffering. It's difficult to see life beyond the pain. If that's you, I challenge you to look up from your circumstances and take stock of the world. Gaze upon the beauty of nature. Stare out upon a few sunrises and sunsets. Listen to the roaring sound of the ocean and life-refreshing gush of a waterfall. Ponder the mysteries of the ecosystem. Spend some time at NASA exploring the marvels of the universe. Then delve into the wonders of the human body. Get a fresh perspective on the endless miracles required for the universe and life as we know it to continue to function. Marvel at the creative, sustaining power behind it all. While you do this, ponder these two questions.

1. If God could bring all this into existence and continue to sustain it, then can't this same God sustain me?

2. Am I willing to trust that God will work all things together for good for those who love God and are called according to His purpose?

It's amazing what the proper perspective can do for you. It is possible to have joy and peace in the midst of suffering. It is possible to be loving and kind in the midst of suffering. It is possible to compassionately care for the needs of others even while you have unmet needs. You are able to maintain a gentle spirit while patiently enduring hardships. In fact, it's in the very act of doing these things that are greatness is demonstrated.

Now, if you happen to be in a period where you feel incredibly blessed with good health, strong relationships, and financial security, you likely see clear waters up ahead. You may have even begun to equate an easy life with God's approval. I also challenge you to look up from your circumstances and take stock of the world. See the pain and suffering that surrounds you and respond with compassion. Allow your heart to be grieved by what you see. Allow your spirit to be broken by the depravity that has enslaved so many. While you do this, ponder these two questions.

1. How I am supposed to use all the resources (money, talents, relationships, etc.) I've been blessed with to address the needs that I see?

2. Am I willing to release everything to God so that God may work through me to accomplish His will and purpose in the lives of others?

It's amazing what the proper perspective can do for you. It is possible to maintain a humble attitude, walk in Godly ambition, and still experience the benefits of economic prosperity. It is possible to have joy and peace and still sacrificially carry the burdens of others. It is possible to be loving, kind, gentle, and inviting to the least of these. In fact, it's in the very act of doing these things that are greatness is demonstrated.

Regardless of where you're standing right now, you can chart a journey toward greatness. It doesn't matter whether you have a little or a lot. It doesn't matter what you're currently experiencing. What matters is whether you're willing to turn your eyes from yourself onto God, and through God onto others. Are you willing to allow God to be Lord over you and all that is "yours" so that it may be used for benefit of others? Nothing else that you do matters unless you've made that initial decision and commit to walking in it. True greatness is not achievable outside of a passionate relationship with God.

EXCERPTS FROM THE POWER OF REST: HOW TO STOP DOING, START BEING, AND SOAR THROUGH LIFE

This book is designed to get you to stop, to slow down your pace, and to live victoriously right where you are; without another position, without another award, and without accumulating another "thing." It's spiritually based leadership at its fullest. At a time when society is saying do more, work as many hours per week as possible, and stay connected 24/7, I'm going to try to sell you on doing less and appreciating it more because you take the time to enjoy it. You will be challenged to commit to less, spend less and focus on less but to do it all with excellence.

This book is all about excelling at what you were designed to do and letting the rest go. You may find yourself challenging your current career aspirations. You may feel led to reinvent your career, engage in entrepreneurship, or create a legacy of people impacted by your service in your current organization. I don't know the exact change that you may want to make, nor can I guarantee that you will change or that your change will be successful. The willingness to change is a personal decision and staying the course through the inevitable ups and downs requires steadfastness. However, I do guarantee that time spent in quiet reflection as you work through this book will reveal aspects of your life that would benefit from change.

You can chose to read and work through this book alone or you can chose to work through this book with others. You can skip ahead to particular chapters that are of interest to you or you can proceed through the book as it is presented. This is your journey, so the path you take is really up to you. My goal is merely to serve as a coach, a mentor, and a guide.

As a coach, I know how important it is to set clear expectations upfront. So before we proceed, let's make sure that we are on the same page as to what you can expect to get from working through the material in this book. First, you should expect to identify opportunities to improve your life, but you should not expect to lay out a plan for a perfect life or for a perfect you. No one is perfect, and no amount of striving will make us perfect.

Second, you should expect to be challenged to transform your life; not just make little tweaks here and there. So the change that we're going to explore is not about becoming the best version of the current you. Rather, the change that we are going to explore is about becoming the person you were always meant to be. It's about letting the passions that have been placed in your heart and the talents and gifts that you've been blessed with shine through like never before. It's about developing authentic and mutually-rewarding relationships with people who are like you and with people who aren't like you. It's about focusing your attention on the things that have lasting value.

Third, this book is focused on you, the individual. However, all of the organizations that you're associated with will also benefit because of your increased capacity for innovation and servant leadership. Your relationships will also benefit. Ultimately, every interaction that you have with other people will improve. A habit of rest truly is that powerful.

I know this because I love to study people. Human behavior is about as fascinating as it comes. I'm an avid reader and have read many fiction books, but there are some things that you just can't make up. Sometimes you hear a real-life story and you can only shake your head, massage your chin, and wonder. Other times, you hear a real-life story and you're pumped out with hope. Their sheer courage and resiliency motivates you to believe the impossible. Why do people have such different stories to share? That's a question that I ponder a lot. As I've studied people over the years, I've come to realize that the people who fail don't set out to fail, and the people who succeed don't have a corner on the talent market.

Printed in the United States
By Bookmasters